HOW TO INVOLVE THE STUDENT

IN CLASSROOM DECISION MAKING

Edited by

William J. Stewart

Associate Professor of Education

University of Northern Iowa

Published by
R & E PUBLISHERS
P. O. Box 2008
Saratoga, California 95070

Library of Congress Card Catalog Number
84-60975

I.S.B.N.
0-88247-737-4

CONTENTS

Page

80203

iv

INTRODUCTION

Pupil-teacher decision making has long been recognized as a worthwhile procedure for adapting instruction to the abilities, interests and needs of pupils. This procedure enables pupils to be involved in planning, carrying out and evaluating their learning experiences. As a result, pupils are more likely to view learning as being interesting and meaningful.

The collection of readings in *HOW TO INVOLVE THE STUDENT IN CLASSROOM DECISION MAKING* is intended to aid and encourage both pre- and in-service teachers in the use of pupil-teacher decision making. These readings support the idea that it is important for teachers to know how to apply pupil-teacher decision making and to be committed to its use. Thus, teachers must not only understand the technique of pupil-teacher decision making, but its historical and theoretical aspects as well. To this end, the readings in this book focus on pupil-teacher decision making in terms of its: historical development, purposes, theoretical principles and practical application.

One premise that underlies the historical development of pupil-teacher decision making is that the degree to which an individual appreciates pupil-teacher decision making is proportionate to that individual's sense of why it developed and how it has changed over the years. Another premise is that an individual can better understand current and evolving pupil-teacher decision making practices once that individual is knowledgeable concerning past practices. Consequently, *HOW TO INVOLVE THE STUDENT IN CLASS-*

1

ROOM DECISION MAKING contains articles that consider the historical development of pupil-teacher decision making.

With any instructional method, it is essential that one be thoroughly familiar with the purposes which that method serves. When one is aware of the functions of pupil-teacher decision making, then he or she can better appreciate its value and, therefore, use it more effectively. In view of this, there are articles in this book that specify the various reasons for making use of pupil-teacher decision making.

Pupil-teacher decision making works best when it is practiced within a sound theoretical framework. This means that the teacher needs to understand and know how to apply the theoretical principles of pupil-teacher decision making. In line with this, articles are included in *HOW TO INVOLVE THE STUDENT IN CLASSROOM DECISION MAKING* that explain pupil-teacher decision making's theoretical principles and how to incorporate them into the instructional system.

The practical application of pupil-teacher decision making relates to the involvement of the pupils in the classroom decision making process. The teacher needs specialized knowledges and skills to put pupil-teacher decision making into practice. For this purpose, articles are included in this book that suggest specific guidelines and approaches for applying pupil-teacher decision making. These articles also set forth both traditional and new pupil-teacher decision making methods.

Successful pupil-teacher decision making necessitates the integration of theory and practice. However, most books on pupil-teacher decision making typically place primary emphasis on the practical application of the procedure. Whereas, this book, through emphasizing both the theory and practice of pupil-teacher decision making, fills an important need in helping teachers to plan with their pupils.

HOW TO INVOLVE THE STUDENT IN CLASSROOM DECISION MAKING can be used in many ways. The text is suitable for use in both undergraduate and graduate courses; in addition, it can be considered a reference book for in-service professionals.

I am deeply grateful to all those who gave permission to reprint the articles included in this book. The friendliness

2

and good wishes so often expressed were most encouraging. It is my hope that *HOW TO INVOLVE THE STUDENT IN CLASSROOM DECISION MAKING* is deserving of their kind responses.

William J. Stewart
Cedar Falls, Iowa

THIS FIRST ARTICLE TELLS WHY IT IS IMPORTANT
TO INVOLVE PUPILS IN GROUP PLANNING. THIS
PLANNING PROCEDURE ALLOWS PUPILS TO COOPER-
ATIVELY DEFINE PROBLEMS, AND DEVISE METHODS
FOR SOLVING THEM. GROUP PLANNING ALSO PRE-
PARES PUPILS TO LIVE IN A DEMOCRATIC SOCIETY
BY PROVIDING EXPERIENCES IN THINKING AND IN
DOING THINGS INDEPENDENTLY. VARIOUS PRIN-
CIPLES ARE OFFERED FOR PUTTING GROUP PLAN-
NING INTO PRACTICE.

IT CAN HAPPEN

H. H. Giles

H. H. Giles, "It Can Happen," *Educational Leadership 1 (4):(January 1944):206-211.* "Reprinted
with permission of the Association for Supervision and Curriculum Development. All rights reserved."

A WISE SUPERVISOR recently remarked, "Surely it
would seem that older students could share in planning and
evaluating their own work since children in the primary
grades do it so well." Her remark was made in reference to
a faculty dispute over methods of teaching. On one side of
that dispute were those who sincerely, earnestly, and a little
bitterly objected to teacher-pupil planning and felt insecure
at the thought of attempting it. They offered arguments to
the effect that it resulted in too much freedom for students,
that standards were lowered, that the orderly process of
subject-matter mastery was disrupted and that only a lazy
teacher would leave it to students to make important decisions.

During the course of the discussion, those who opposed the method of group planning, work and evaluation at the elementary level raised objections and questions like these:

"The children run wild."

"When do they learn the three R's?"

"What would the next teacher say if my students were not required to cover certain minimum essentials?"

"I just don't believe in it!"

"Parents want their children to go to a teacher who knows something, not to a teacher who has to ask help from her pupils."

"It may work for some people, but it doesn't work for me. I tried it for several weeks and I can't teach that way."

"The administration doesn't approve of it."

These objections and questions were heart-felt and were expressed with the tone of voice which implies, "I dare you to prove me wrong!" During the hot dispute, a professor of science rose to assert:

"When students are given a share in planning, they choose things which interest them rather than what is good for them. To give boys and girls academic credit for having a good time rather than following the course of study is downright dishonest!"

This particular discussion was more heated than others, perhaps, but it was one of many in the institution referred to and is representative of several things which are worth serious study and reply.

Where Do You Stand?

Consider the assertion, "I don't believe in it!" Any number of people do not believe in cooperative planning. All who believe in authoritarianism are against it. Group planning which invites all members to participate in defining problems and methods of attacking them is a denial of external authority and an affirmation of faith in the intelligence of those present. There are many elements in our culture which are opposed to the belief in the development of all through participation in thinking. Graduate schools do not generally invite their students to practice group planning; political parties do not open their inner councils to all the membership; high school and grade school teachers rely to a considerable extent on the authority of a textbook; and parents in many cases feel free to impose their will "because I say so."

This is a serious matter because these are times in which the authoritarian position is crucial in the world. If the war has any meaning whatever, it is found in the issue of authoritarianism, of special privilege for some, as opposed to the participation and free development of all.

Therefore, the teacher who does not believe in pupil participation in thinking about why, what, and how to use school time is quite in line with the authoritarian concepts which, both in the past and the present, have dominated life and education in much of the world. That teacher is true to the accepted pattern of training in paternalistic homes and in classical education.

It is not many years since the idea of "learning by doing" was elaborated into a philosophy by John Dewey, though the practice is as old as man, particularly outside of formal education. Its effectiveness is one reason why employers have preferred workers who learned on the job. Yet American education, supposedly democratic, has frequently provided the spectacle of large-scale efforts to "teach" without offering pupils experience in thinking or in doing things for themselves.

Ask Yourself. . .

Thus, for the teacher who inquires concerning effective methods of education, there are two questions raised:

(1)   Do you truly believe in the ability of every human being to grow?

(2)   Do you believe that growth takes place most efficiently through first-hand experience?

If the answer is No to the first of these, then rigid standards and preconceived ideas of course content are a natural result, for the aim of education becomes in a large measure the weeding-out of the unfit.

If the answer is No to the second of these, then lectures and textbooks become ends in themselves. Memorization and regurgitation are elevated to a high position. The humble, faltering, often unexpected results of practical experiments in group thinking and work are made to seem reprehensible rather than educational.

If these questions are answered affirmatively; if the teacher has real faith in the ability of all to grow, and in the value of first-hand experience, then there yet remain many difficulties. Democracy is not easy! Some of the difficulties are indicated by the following questions:

"How can the teacher plan with the children to get the things they need?"

"What differences in procedure are necessary for different age levels?"

"Wouldn't it be better to learn the facts and skills first — then apply them?"

"How do you avoid substituting the guidance of leading students for that of the teacher?"

"How can you give grades on the basis of individual progress rather than on standard tests and group norms?"

"What is the place of books and other traditional materials of learning in group-planned teachings?"

8

"What kind of pre-planning is necessary?"

An Adventure in Discovery

To such questions as these there are some general answers which may be of service. But it can be said with confidence that there are no final answers which will apply equally to every case. The democratic way of life and education supposes unique qualities in individual human beings, unique factors in situations, and unique solutions to problems. It does not lend itself to fixed and easy answers. Thus the process of growth in the classroom is a perpetual adventure in new discovery of the uses of intelligence. The generalizations which are to be given here must be continually changed as teachers and pupils discover new interests and capabilities.

At present, it seems well warranted from the experience of scores of groups to make the following general statement in answer to the questions above.

Group planning is most successful when it is preceded by a period of work, assigned by the teacher, during which all members of the group get acquainted and establish a basis for mutual respect. When group planning begins, experience shows that it is most effective where the following conditions exist:

1.   Extensive and careful pre-planning by the teacher, including careful thinking about purpose, worthwhile topics, limitations, and possibilities of material and personnel.

2.   Use of the pre-planning chiefly as a basis for questions which will stimulate student thinking rather than to provide quick answers.

3.   A teacher attitude (based on faith in the potential growth of ability of students) which invites genuine and widespread participation.

4.   A wide variety of problems and purposes of

study explored.

5. A final determination of study area broad enough to include the real interests of all members of the group.

6. A clear definition of the major and minor study areas, so carefully thought out that intensive work is demanded for the solution of vital problems.

7. Use of all the available resources of the environment which are most pertinent to the problem; e.g., printed materials, laboratories, radio and other news sources, people of experience in the field.

8. Continuous planning and evaluation as the work progresses, and changes made as the actual work proves them necessary. (This means providing students with opportunity and encouragement to re-think their purposes and procedures and to state new ideas frankly.)

9. Evaluation which takes into account the original purpose, the achievement of the group as a whole, and the contributions of individuals of all types and degrees of importance.

Responsibility and Growth

To state these principles more specifically in relation to the questions given: The teacher has a responsibility for knowing how to plan, what sources of information are available, what the students are like, and what the difficulties and limitations may be. Some of this information will come from previous experience, but much from the actual process of planning and from observing a particular group of children at work.

In the case of young children, the planning and discussions may be briefer, the responsibilities less heavy than with older students. But, in either case, the big point is to find out all the ideas the children have to give them the experience of weighing them and trying out their ideas, to help them see greater meanings and possibilities by skillful questions, silences, suggestions, uses of material, time, and space.

As age and experience increase, so will the possibilities of work and of independent responsibility. But at all ages, children have genuine interests, worries, and abilities. As Comenius said, "everything in its time." The good teacher knows each child, knows the temper of the group as such, strives to be an artist in the timing of activities. The good teacher is a fellow student to pupils, a fellow student whose greater knowledge of techniques is used to aid development, but is not used to supplant first-hand discovery. The good teacher does not attempt to impose by force either the rate or the direction of internal growth.

The teacher who listens to children hears many questions which can become the basis for study. Some are about themselves, some about the great world. All of them can lead to the use of many methods of work, many kinds of materials for study, many forms of presenting results, serious effort to judge results accurately and to continue planning more effectively.

Living as the Course of Study

Many of the things children "really need" are the things which children already are asking questions about when the classroom is a happy, free place where all respect each other as persons. The problems of daily life are the true course of study. Science and arts materials are aids to solving these problems. Facts and skills are acquired best as the natural result of genuine desire to accomplish a purpose, to solve a real problem.

If students are capable of thinking and directing themselves, it is stultifying to their growth to deny them the opportunity. If the problems for study are real to the students, they will impose their own discipline, approaching the problem with clear understanding and effective use of materials and techniques. Who shall say what is a real and challenging problem to a student better than he himself?

In a sense, it is almost absurd that it should be necessary to urge schoolteachers to give their pupils opportunity to think. Yet that is what is being done by this argument for student-teacher planning. It is precisely the purpose of group planning to increase the extent, the depth, and the desire to think: the desire, by making the pupil a responsible partner in the job of relating his study to his interests, curiosities, problems, and previous experience; the depth, by the demands which a real problem rather than an artificial, teacher or text-dictated problem make; the extent, by facing the student with the task of defining as far as possible for himself the Why and the How of his problems, instead of doing this hard work for him. The extent, also, by making clear how scientific method, concepts of quantity and relation, the recorded thoughts of man—all the material now divided into subject fields (for the convenience of the specialist)—can be applied to the understanding and solution of problems in the daily living of each of us.

There is no issue concerning the idea that problem solving is the basis of mental and emotional development. There seems to be an issue as to whether an outside authority or a pupil and his teacher best know what problems are real and important to a pupil at a given moment.

If there are doubts as to the validity of the idea that all growth and development are highly personal in form and meaning, there are now available a number of sound, substantiating studies.[1] If there are doubts regarding the validity of starting with a whole problem instead of with facts and skills, other studies can answer them.[2] If there are doubts concerning the ability and responsibility of students thus challenged to think for themselves, see the record of youth in the war and the testimony of teachers who have described their work in current educational journals.[3]

Look About You

Or, look about you. In the rural county of Georgia where the author now lives, as formerly in the large city high

12

schools he has observed, children choose important things to do when they are given opportunity and wise, friendly help. Examples from the schools of this county are many.

Here is a first grade which has committees for cleaning the room and which produces plays, sings folk songs, counts money; a fifth grade which runs a cooperative store; a seventh-eight grade which plans hot lunch menus; a ninth grade which builds a lunchroom, makes a community survey, plants a school garden, paints its classroom, and builds play equipment; a fifth-sixth grade which investigates the costs and design and successfully aids in the promotion of a cooperative sweet potato curing house and plants grass and shrubs; a seventh-eight grade which studies avidly our neighbors in South America, makes extensive study of local health problems, establishes a school clinic, and works on malaria control.

Though it is never easy to promote the maximum growth of all students, even in schools where weather conditions and the frequent moving of tenant farmer families cause irregular attendance, these activities go on and are testimony to the fact that through shared thinking, there is intellectual adventure and rich practical results. The precise details of method will vary with the teacher's knowledge and skill. Basically, the method is as simple as asking the following questions, effective and continuously:

What, Who, and When?

What do we need to do? What do we need to know? Who should do what, when? What do we need to work with? How shall we divide the tasks? Who can help us most?

And—as the job is under way and when it is done— What was well done? What was not so well done? What did we get out of it? What next?

It has been the experience of many teachers that students take these questions seriously and seek answers eagerly and effectively, according to their actual ability and experience. The most difficult part of the job is probably to overcome a long training in the belief that the teacher must do the thinking for students. Another difficulty is to find ways of reaching all the students and getting discussion started. Here is where careful pre-planning can provide many stimulating leads in the form of questions which will pique interest and lead to serious consideration of values.

What Can We Expect?

Finally, the method of group planning is rarely 100 percent successful. It is likely to show very plainly who the loafers and non-cooperators are. In fact, it seems to reveal weaknesses more than other methods, where as one administrator put it, "Seventy percent of the students get by through doing a minimum of work and keeping quiet." When an individual is responsible for carrying out part of a group plan and does not do so, the results are highlighted. This is probably a good thing because it shows the teacher where her greatest efforts must be put.

In addition, it is doubtful whether any method whatever is more than 70 to 80 percent effective at a given time. As has been pointed out, human development is a highly individual matter and schools in general require a good deal of group treatment. The expectations of parents and of schools themselves are often beyond the possibilities. The aim of democracy—the maximum development of all—requires a long, difficult process of growth. It requires the utmost application of science and art on the part of the teacher and it is the only social idea which aims so high.

The methods of democracy, particularly the means of obtaining general participation in thinking, are far from well-established. It requires, therefore, a pioneer spirit and the secure foundation of a concerted belief on the part of a faculty group to put this high ideal into practical operation. It is easier to follow in the traditional paths of authoritarianism. Only the teacher who truly believes in the goal should even begin the attempt to make the classroom a place for adventures in cooperative thinking and original discovery. But for that teacher who believes in democarcy, group planning has possibilities. It can happen.

References

[1]Allport, Gordon: *Personality, A Psychological Interpretation*, New York: Henry Holt, 1937.

Plant, J. S.: *Personality and the Cultural Pattern*, New York: The Commonwealth Fund, 1937.

"The Child, the Clinic and the Court," *New Republic*, New York, 1925.

Rogers, C. R.: *Psychotherapy, A Method of Counseling*. Boston: Houghton Mifflin, 1942.

[2]Wheeler, R. H., and Perkins, F. T.: *Principles of Mental Development*. New York: Thomas Y. Crowell, 1932.

[3]See also the list of questions recorded by one teacher of junior high school social science (Giles, H.H.: *Teacher-Pupil Planning*, New York: Harper, 1941, pp. 259-284) and "University School. An Inventory of the Personal and General Social Problems of 256 Students in Grades Seven to Twelve Inclusive." Columbus, Ohio: Ohio State University School, 1940.

THE AUTHOR OF THE NEXT ARTICLE POINTS OUT
HOW PUPIL-TEACHER PLANNING PROVIDES PUPILS
WITH THE ATTITUDES AND SKILLS THAT ARE NEEDED
TO SUCCESSFULLY PARTICIPATE IN THE DEMO-
CRATIC WAY OF LIFE. THE PUPILS ARE INVOLVED,
THROUGH PUPIL-TEACHER PLANNING, IN AUTHEN-
TIC CLASSROOM EXPERIENCES IN COOPERATIVE LIV-
ING. THE AUTHOR INDICATES HOW PUPIL-TEACHER
PLANNING CAN BE APPLIED AT THE ELEMENTARY,
JUNIOR HIGH AND HIGH SCHOOL LEVELS.

TEACHER — PUPIL PLANNING

John F. Rios

*Reprinted from Arizona Teacher-Parent, Vol. 39,
No. 3 (Spring 1951), pp. 18 + 29, by permission
of the Arizona Education Association.*

Youth subjected to autocratic teaching can never learn
the way of living called democracy. Since, as teachers, it is
our special responsibility to further democratic living, our
problem becomes one of developing teaching procedures
which will equip young citizens to participate in that way of
life.

As long as the American people strive to improve and
perpetuate our way of life, our teaching methods will continue to change. One of our newest methods, teacher-pupil
planning, seeks to create within the classroom genuine experiences in cooperative living. In the curriculum improvement process, two very significant trends have emerged:[1]
(1) More attempts have been made to organize around
themes, processes, centers of interest, and problems, rather
than subject matter. (2) Pupils participating more in select-

ing their curriculum experiences.

Contrary to considerable erroneous thought, teacher-pupil planning is much more than meeting the class and asking, "What would you like to do today?" Pre-planning is a must and increases as pupils are given more and more opportunity to participate.

The Role of the Principal

In considering the principal's role in teacher-pupil planning, we first examine the basic concept of our society. Our nation is great because it has been built on the idea of freedom for man in as practical a way as man has known how to fashion it. The tone of our freedom is set by the personality adjustment of the individuals that make up our democracy.[2]

The function of the principal is to help improve the program by collecting facts, enlisting staff judgment, and accepting plans for change in terms of the judgments made.

In moving in the direction of democratic organization within the school, the teacher and principal often experience a feeling of insecurity. Testing new patterns of teaching requires an adventurous courage, backed by the same qualities of concern for the welfare of all that is manifested in a good home for the members of the family. The principal must become a guide and helper, inspiring confidence in his staff as they strive to reveal the true interest of life to boys and girls.

Less Vagueness

Getting pupils to participate in the hard, intellectual discipline of thinking together with the teacher requires less vagueness and more planning than do many teacher-dictated assignments.

In the first phase of planning, the teacher will need to select a variety of topics to be suggested indirectly to the students for possible use. The second phase may be thought of as the stage-setting. Inasmuch as physical surroundings do affect the feelings and attitudes of students, the classroom should be attractive. All equipment should be easily adjustable for the purposes it is to serve; tables, cabinets, and library facilities must be accessible.

The third phase includes general group discussion and individual as well as small group study with a good balance between seat work and free movement. Of extreme importance is the opportunity for the pupil to report his progress to the group.

Evaluation of accomplishment will be made by the entire group but should be provided for by the teacher. Various means may be used such as checklists, questionnaires, oral presentations, and so forth.

When these five steps have been carefully pre-planned by the teacher, all is in readiness for planning with the children.

At the Primary Level

The primary teacher is with her pupils all day and comes to know each child extremely well. She has a rather free hand as to the methods of teaching she uses. Since there are no strict departmental areas to limit time, the teacher can combine and arrange subject matter as she sees fit.

Teacher-pupil planning starts at the beginning of the school year with problems of immediate interest to all the children. This may include the best ways of carrying on routine activities, handling messages, receiving visitors, caring for the library, and arranging table displays.

A unit of work may be organized around first-hand experiences of the children. The teacher must have a general plan of the unit with a wide variety of resource materials to challenge the interest of every child and to involve as many learning experiences as possible.

This planning develops skills, knowledge, attitudes, ideals, and social responsibility.

In the Junior High School

Teacher-pupil planning in the junior high school substitutes real learning by experience for the appearance of learning by doing what the teacher says. It presents a way for the teacher to enrich and clarify the learning program.

The teacher must be prepared to meet with many difficulties. Adolescents familiar with regimentation and authoritarian methods are likely to misunderstand any new-found freedom. Good academic students without leadership abilities, timid introvertive students, and other types which cannot adjust to the group will resent this change which might lower their status. Therefore, the teacher should look upon himself as a group leader, who employs students to develop their own experiences. In order to fulfill this aim, the teacher will need to provide work for the weak, use local material, expect and ask for sacrifices, start early, provide novelty, and delegate as much detail as possible.[3]

This planning makes the pupils perceptive, critical, and appreciative.

In the Senior High School

Teacher-pupil planning at the senior high school level aims at developing initiative and the ability to think independently, both of which are qualities needed by young people preparing to take their places as adult citizens in our democracy.

But here, too, the teacher must take care that the planning begins at the level of the pupils' ability to think out problems and to work together cooperatively. In groups that have not been allowed to share in the responsibility of choosing their own problem areas, it is probably wise to begin with the simple planning of an occasional field trip, asking speakers who are authorities in their field to talk to the group, listening to the radio, using all kinds of visual aids, or reading from many sources.

Cooperative community planning, in which teachers, students and adults work together, is the logical extension of teacher-pupil planning in high school.[4] Civic improvement, a student employment bureau, income tax service, or a Christmas shoppers' nursery are just a few of the many projects that might be pursued.[5]

This program is applicable to any school dedicated to the development of worthwhile social attitudes in its young people.

Conclusion
Several research studies which have been made to support the value of teacher-pupil planning and to substantiate the belief that through this method pupils learn the attitudes and skills of cooperative living. Pupils who participate in this plan display better social adjustments, show more consideration of others, are more objective in evaluating the results of individual and group processes, are more sensitive to the values of contributions of others, and demonstrate a greater willingness to accept responsibility.

Teacher-pupil planning is one of the best known methods of educating our youth for life adjustments.

References

[1] Report of the Thirteenth Annual Conference-Laboratory on Problems of Curriculum and Instruction at The University of Texas, p. 11.

[2] Giles, H. H. *Teacher-Pupil Planning*, p. 16.

[3] Hoag, Victor, *It's Fun To Teach*, p. 100.

[4] Alberty, Harold, *Reorganizing The High School Curriculum*, p. 350.

[5] *Parker High School Serves Its People*, pp. 65-76.

NEXT IS AN ARTICLE THAT EXPLAINS HOW EIGHTH
GRADE PUPILS ACCEPTED RESPONSIBILITY FOR CO-
OPERATIVELY PLANNING THEIR LEARNING ACTIVI-
TIES FOR THE SCHOOL YEAR. THE INVOLVEMENT OF
THE PUPILS IN PUPIL-TEACHER PLANNING ENABLED
THEM TO EXPERIENCE SIGNIFICANT ACADEMIC,
EMOTIONAL AND SOCIAL GROWTH. THE ARTICLE
MENTIONS SPECIFIC WAYS IN WHICH THE PUPILS
WERE ABLE TO PLAN, CARRY OUT AND EVALUATE
THEIR LEARNING ACTIVITIES.

TOGETHER WE DEFINE PURPOSES

Katie I. Misaka

*Katie I. Misaka, "Together We Define Purposes,"
Educational Leadership 17 (1):(October 1959):
11-15.* "Reprinted with permission of the Association for Supervision and Curriculum Development. Copyright © 1959 by the Association for
Supervision and Curriculum Development. All
rights reserved.

Much of what has been written in education in recent
years establishes the desirability of involving children and
youth in the planning of the school experiences. Some of
our beliefs about working with children in the teaching-
learning process are that an individual:

1.   Learns as a whole

2.   Is in a constant process of change

3.   Is motivated by a drive for self-enhancement

4. Behaves in accordance with his self-perception

5. Learns best what has meaning and purpose for him

6. Is led to self-commitment and self-direction by the internalization of goals

7. Works best in an atmosphere of acceptance

8. Is more productive if he is able to accept himself and others

9. Learns to value democratic purposes through democratic methods.

These and other assumptions provide the framework, then, for classroom practices.

Planning Activities

Students in one eighth grade core class were invited to participate in planning their learning activities for the school year. Each was asked (a) what kind of person he would like to be, and (b) what skills and knowledge he believed were essential for him during and by the end of the eighth grade. During class discussion, the teacher wrote the students' ideas on the board while the secretary recorded them in the class notebook.

Proponents of each idea met with other interested persons to look further at possible content and activities. Brief reports of their recommendations were given to the class. The group established some criteria for deciding which suggestions seemed to be most valuable:

1. Will the knowledge and experiences be useful?

2. Will the knowledge and experiences increase our understanding of democracy?

3.   Will the knowledge and experiences be of interest to everyone?

4.   Are there adequate resource persons and materials available?

After deliberation, it was decided that the group goals for the year would include:

1.   Learning about ourselves as adolescents

2.   Increasing our skills in communication (speaking, listening, reading, writing [to include spelling])

3.   Increasing our knowledge of America's history

4.   Learning what the bases are of American democracy

5.   Increasing in appreciation of and skill in sports, both as spectator and as participant

6.   Learning to control emotions, develop poise

7.   Learning better interviewing techniques and telephone courtesy

8.   Learning more about world problems as they relate to the United States.

It was suggested next that a priority order be established. The consensus was, however, that all of the goals were important, and that if time and activities were planned thoughtfully, the students would be able to deal in some manner with all of them during the year. It became obvious that some of the goals were continuing and would become a part of almost every activity, but others, such as American history, would lend themselves to more organized study. These teenagers began by learning about themselves.

They also agreed to spend a half-hour three days per week reading for pleasure; one hour two days per week investigating current issues in the news. Other activities for which time was budgeted were daily business, student government discussions, and specific skill development. For example, various students found it necessary to gain further mastery of interviewing techniques, letter forms, use of the dictionary, outlining procedures, and formation of plurals. This left the major part of the two periods for more focused work on the general problem.

Each day, or as often as necessary, the total group, small groups, or individuals made plans for action. Almost every day an agenda was built. Occasionally the teacher asked the class what needed to be done that day. Sometimes she listed items which had been agreed upon and asked the class to establish priority. At times an individual volunteered to propose agenda items subject to class approval. Often the needs of the ongoing work committee determined the schedule.

In addition to the group planning, an opportunity was provided for students to make individual commitments. On occasion the teacher listed the major tasks of the day across the board and invited students to sign up. At times commitments were made orally. Sometimes pupils wrote out an individual plan for action. Each plan included the nature of the task, with whom it was to be executed (sometimes alone, of course), the activities involved, the materials needed, the amount of time necessary. To the teacher this individual pupil planning seemed time very profitably spent, for she was then able to serve as resource person, guide, challenger. When a student needed help to budget time, to find materials, and the like, the teacher was free to assist. Then the boy or girl was off on his own again, his steps clear.

As the year progressed, the third goal, "increasing our knowledge of America's history," became the major problem area. In this classroom, as in all others in the school, there were copies of many texts and other reference materials. To illustrate, these students made use of 20 different texts ranging from 5th to 12th grade levels. The school library furnished numerous other books. Since some pupils needed help in locating and recording the main ideas in their reading, time was set aside that week to develop these specific skills. Issues of the *READ* magazine were particularly helpful as they were focusing on outlining skills during this time. Students practiced outlining their historical references which then were evaluated by student and teacher. As some gained competence, they began to look for other ways of recording information, although some preferred the outline.

During the study of American history, a discussion of some of the issues debated by the authors of the U. S. Constitution took an unusual turn. The group decided to set up a hypothetical "colony" on another planet and to write a constitution. Since the students in the class would be the first inhabitants, their values would determine the laws of the group. Each person, including the teacher, was to think over very carefully and to write down as clearly as possible what he considered his major values in life. These stated values were compiled by a committee of three chosen by the group. Later individuals volunteered to work on committees to investigate and to clarify social, religious, economic and political beliefs as well as individual rights. A chairman of the "constitutional convention" was elected, as were a "scribe" and a "sergeant-at-arms". This work received further impetus when the children read in *LIFE* magazine that a group of people in Michigan were meeting in a basement room to establish rules for living together as they proceeded in a caravan to Alaska and after they arrived.

Several factors served to keep individual student participation at a high level at the "convention." Participation charts were kept, sometimes by the teacher and sometimes by volunteers from the group. One day the class discussed what happens when one or two members dominate. In addition to stimulating participation, the chairman was adept at keeping the focus. He used phrases such as "I believe we were discussing. . ."; or "That's an important idea, too, Joe, but shall we answer Katherine's questions first?"

The Unexpected Happens
The search for common beliefs made students examine

and clarify their values. This aroused emotions and caused tension to mount as conflicting values were recognized and worked through.

As discussion began one morning under the direction of the convention chairman, one of the boys said, "I've been thinking this over and, well, first, I want to say that I believe in representative government and agree with most of the things that we have said so far, but I think it will be better if we start out with a strong leader."

"How strong is 'strong'?" one of the girls asked.

"I think he should have a lot of authority and take charge to see that everything gets organized. Then after we get our basic problems solved, well, then, we can afford to be more democratic."

The teacher was stunned. Two or three students nodded assent and murmured, "That's what I think." One of the boys said, "If you do that, Stephen, then you're admittine that democracy won't work."

"No, I'm not, I think it will work, but I'm just saying that democracy is slow and inefficient! If we're going to be settling a new land, we have to get going faster, that's all."

Some students looked at the teacher. By this time there was general buzzing among the class members. Sides appeared to be forming. It began to look as if democracy might lose. One of the boys who had been on the "political beliefs" committee said, "Okay, okay. Now look. Our committee talked over all the different forms of government. We had a lot of arguments, but we think we chose the best parts from all of them. We think that the best kind of government is the one we proposed. Stephen, do you want to go against that?"

"Well, as you know, I didn't agree with some of the things the committee said. I just wanted to be able to express my opinion." Discussion ensued. Should a committee member go along with the majority vote or should he be allowed to dissent in public? The class agreed that a committee report should indicate the minority opinion also, if it were sufficiently strong.

The chairman re-focused the discussion on authoritarian vs. democratic government. The role of a leader was

27

reviewed. (The group had described the leadership role earlier in the year.) The teacher came into the discussion to ask the group to consider the relationship of practices to the achievement of objectives. The situation was finally resolved. The class agreed that the strong leader meant an extremely capable person who did have a very important duty, but whose powers would always be determined by the other colonists. Furthermore, the responsibility for efficient organization belonged to everyone.

Work Is Evaluated

As each problem area during the year was brought to a solution, students evaluated the group's efforts as well as their own. Discussion to see whether group golas had been achieved focused on these questions which were developed by the group:

What were our objectives?

Did we accomplish them?

What objective was of particular interest to you?

Were you interested in your share of the activities?

In what skills do you feel you have improved?

What new skills have you gained?

Did the group improve in its skill in working together?

What subject matter fields did we draw upon?

What would you change if you were to plan this unit again?

In December the group discussed the characteristics of a well-rounded eighth grader. Letters of self-evaluation were written by students to their parents covering the topics of personality, friendships, physical well-being, participation in school activities, self-direction, study skills, leading-out and general knowledge.

A report to parents consisting of a checklist of behavioral goals of the school plus written statements was sent home by the teacher three times during the year. Examples from the checklist are: demonstrates a growing ability and insight in analyzing situations and problems which he faces and in reacting appropriately to them; shows growth in ability to phrase a request, to organize ideas, to present a point of view, to relate an experience.

Learning More About Students

The teacher attempted to provide opportunity for students to "feed-back" their feelings about what was going on in the classroom. Such questions as "How did you feel about our progress today?" or "When Hugh said, . . ., what meaning did you give to it?" Part of the time students handed in written reactions. More often the group members discussed their feelings.

By means of a checklist, the teacher asked for students' perceptions of her as a helper. Some students wanted to know how they were perceived by their classmates. Those who wrote their names on the blackboard at a given time received brief, written reactions from all other members in the class. These reactions were compiled by the teacher and a private conference was held with each student. Generally, three points were discussed (a) summary of the reactions, (b) feelings about the perceptions, and (c) steps necessary for maintaining the relationship or changing the relationship.

Pupils also wrote on "What Kind of a Boy (Girl) I Think I Am." They wrote on "What I Think the Teacher Thinks of Me." In addition, personal problems checklists and writing that the group did during their work on understanding adolescence provided further data.

In summary, we have said that:

1.   One can have confidence in the quality of the decisions if students know that with the teacher they are

responsible for making choices in the planning, the follow-through and the evaluating of their school experiences.

2. Goals tend to become internalized and lead to self-commitment and self-direction if students share in goal-setting.

3. Students are eager to study subject matter and improve their study skills if the need for this study and these skills grows out of purposeful experiences.

4. The real concerns and values of each individual must be understood by himself and by the teacher if they are to work toward common goals.

5. Self-evaluation is necessary if objectives are to be achieved.

6. Democratic values can be strengthened if the classroom is operated democratically.

THE AUTHOR OF THE FOLLOWING ARTICLE DE-
SCRIBES HOW THE TEACHER AND PUPILS CAN CO-
OPERATIVELY PLAN EXPERIENCE UNITS. THE PUPILS,
AS THEY PARTICIPATE IN PLANNING EXPERIENCE
UNITS, BECOME MORE MOTIVATED TO TAKE RE-
SPONSIBILITY FOR THEIR LEARNING. SPECIFIC PRO-
CEDURES ARE OUTLINED FOR INVOLVING PUPILS IN
PLANNING EXPERIENCE UNITS.

CONSTRUCTING AN EXPERIENCE UNIT

Sister Aloysius Clare Maher

*Reprinted from Grade Teacher, October 1962.
Copyright © 1962 by Macmillan Professional
Magazines. Used by permission of The Instructor
Publications, Inc.*

What is an experience unit? Experience unit, unit of
work, activity unit are different terms for the same concept.

An experience unit is a segment of experience which is
cut out for study and within which method is employed. It
is based upon the daily and practical life experiences in which
children are interested. In an experience unit, the teacher and
the pupils cooperate in planning the experiences. This teacher-pupil planning has many advantages which enhance the
teaching-learning situation in the classroom. When children
have a part in the planning, they take a new look at subject
matter; they are more interested in the outcomes, they strive
to achieve the goals of learning which they have set up under
the guidance of the teacher; they take on responsibility for
tasks and activities assigned, they are helped to develop desirable attitudes socially and mentally; they develop habits of
industry, ideas, appreciations, understandings and essential

skills and abilities.

Experience units usually grow out of child interest; that is, the activities of the class must grow out of the immediate, day-to-day interests of children. This is well and good, but pupil interests need the guidance of a competent teacher or they become chaotic and meaningless. It is the lasting and enduring interests of children with which we are concerned, not with their changing immediate interests.

Can a teacher preplan the experience unit since it grows out of the interests of children? Yes, a unit may be safely preplanned by the teacher. It is the teacher's job to examine carefully the value of a unit, to note the opportunities for experiencing which it affords, to define clearly the aims of the unit, and to know in advance the materials of instruction which will be needed for the activities planned. Every teacher should know where her class is going and how it will get there.

The unit on "How We Use Arithmetic in the Daily Newspaper" was preplanned in part. The deluge of "Back-to-School" advertisements and "Summer Sales" in the local newspapers stimulated the development of a unit around numbers in the daily paper. Arithmetic is not universally liked by fourth-graders, especially at the beginning of the school year. Then, too, the teacher is anxious to know where to begin after vacation experiences have crowded out some previous learning experiences. The idea of a colorful bulletin board with sample advertisements was considered a good way to determine the interest of children in numbers. The "experience nook" in the classroom was another eye-catcher. An adequate amount of instructional materials is an aid in making this an ideal starting point.

The enthusiastic teacher never misses an opportunity to observe and listen to reactions of pupils as they cluster around a bulletin board the first days of school. The experience of buying school supplies, clothing, lunch boxes, and so forth, is an experience common to all the children. This fact, that it is something which revolves around their daily lives, elicits their wholehearted cooperation with the teacher and enables her to provide for individual differences which will appear during the course of the unit development.

In the first planning period, under the guidance of the teacher, children's responses are listed and their knowledge of arithmetical vocabulary is fully explored. The teacher knows clearly her objectives — general and specific — for the teaching-learning activities. She realizes that the children have goals, too. Therefore, she carefully helps the children to coordinate and integrate their goals with her aims. The varied activities, which are suggested in the newspaper unit, will be enriched and extended by other suggestions which the children will introduce in their group planning.

It is wise and advantageous for the teacher to incorporate each child's ideas. Then in the final plan for activities, those ideas which are duplicates or which overlap may be eliminated. In this way, each child will feel that he is accepted by the group and by the teacher, and he will be fired with a spark of success from the beginning.

The problem solving activities, the creative and constructive experiences, the practice of the development of skills in the unit do not differ from the procedure used in any other subject unit.

The amount of time to be utilized in the development and completion of this unit will differ according to the knowleged which the children demonstrate. The unit, if used during the first few weeks of school, should prove very helpful to the teacher, should be novel to the children, removed from the monotonous drill of the textbook, and should develop desirable attitudes toward arithmetic — the wanting to learn more and more about numbers and how they function in our daily life, and the application of learning activities to present and future life situations.

IN THE NEXT ARTICLE, THE AUTHOR SPECIFIES HOW
THE ABILITIES, DESIRES AND NEEDS OF PUPILS ARE
MET THROUGH PUPIL-TEACHER PLANNING. THE
ARTICLE EXPLAINS HOW THE THRUST OF PUPIL-
TEACHER PLANNING IS TOWARD INDIVIDUALIZA-
TION OF INSTRUCTION. FIFTEEN SUGGESTIONS ARE
PROVIDED FOR ENABLING PUPILS AND TEACHERS
TO PLAN, WORK AND EVALUATE TOGETHER.

PUPIL-TEACHING PLANNING

James H. Young

*Reprinted from Catholic School Journal, Vol.
69, No. 9 (November 1969), pp. 38-42, by permission of the author.*

Teachers, curriculum planners and administrators
seem to be searching for ways to involve students in curriculum planning at various levels of the educational scheme.

If we think of curriculum not as a course of study, but
rather as all the experiences and activities planned under the
aegis of the school and fulfilled by the joint and cohesive
efforts of teachers and learners — not to exclude teachers as
learners — then it would seem that a stronger and more complex thread must connect curriculum and the methods by
which students are helped to learn through involvement in
that curriculum. The slightness with which this connection
has been made is becoming a major concern of teachers because they can hardly be expected to fulfill the objectives of
any curriculum if they are unaware of and lack the necessary
skills to implement the variety of techniques which can effectively improve such a process.

Decision Making

Once the teacher is aware of the complexities of teaching methods, he must become a decision maker in order to select the correct method for meeting certain objectives and alternate methods in meeting other objectives. The impact upon teachers of the variety of methods, techniques and skills needed to successfully implement the curriculum is certainly great. This decision making becomes crucial when the objectives of a curriculum have anything to do with individualization of instruction in a democratic process.

The one democratically-oriented, student-involving methodology that is often forgotten and rarely taught (or practiced for that matter) by teachers is that of pupil-teacher planning.

Pupil-teacher planning means that educational activities are planned carefully with students so that their desires, needs and abilities are fully considered. Students and teachers plan, work and evaluate together to meet their objectives in a specific learning situation to solve a common problem.

Pupil-teacher planning by no means indicates that students tell the teacher how or what to teach. Neither does it imply that the teacher walks into her room daily and says, "What shall we do today, students?"

Students have to be taught to plan, just as they must be taught any other skill or set of skills. The teaching of planning normally begins with an over-balance of direction from the teacher and eventually obtains a relatively equal balance of teacher and student planned activity. In its fully developed stage it has an overbalance of planning, activity and evaluation done by students, with the teacher serving only as a guiding hand.

Perhaps one of the reasons for neglecting the teaching and application of this methodology is the fact that the criteria by which good teacher-pupil planning can be identified are rarely found in usable form. The methodology is classified here into behavioral suggestions followed by an explanation of each so that the teacher can select behaviors appropriate to her needs. In no instance should the behavioral suggestions be construed as specific directions; rather they might better be viewed as suggestions from which the teacher can filter out those he needs to meet specific objectives that are couched in a desirable democratic framework.

1. In pupil-teacher planning, the teacher insures that all participants in this process know one another.

    Students get acquainted through the normal course of events, but the teacher can foster this through the use of simple name and related information-building games. The teacher, further, must constantly seek information about each student. He can gain evidence from anecdotal records, standardized tests, sociograms, formal and informal classroom activities and conferences.

2. The teacher uses abilities and leadership qualities of students to solve problems.

    This process helps establish class rapport and affords opportunities for students to gain respect for abilities and skills of individual classmates. Students, regardless of the level of ability, should be encouraged to display skills that could profit the group. Even the student who seemingly has no other contribution to make except, for example, playing the guitar, should be drawn into appropriate activities. This particular student could contribute significantly to lessons in math (musical time, length of strings), science (sound), social studies (music of different cultures) and a host of other areas.

    An intermediate step in pupil-teacher planning would be to involve students in planning a specific lesson. Questions such as: What is our problem? What information do we need to work out an answer to the problem? and Where can we find such information? can serve to build a solid foundation for more extensive pupil-teacher planning. Thus the planning is initiated on a small scale and works to larger boundaries at a later stage of development.

3. The rationale for using pupil-teacher planning must be understood by students.

   This is a long-term process geared to develop an understanding of, and appreciation for the skills necessary for democratic living. The teacher must help students understand the logic of this technique and develop attitudes conducive to fulfillment of planned objectives. Students must be guided to understand that courses of action can be determined and responsible decisions can be shared through pupil-teacher planning. They can also gain a keen understanding regarding correlation of subject matter, skills and ideals.

4. Detail pre-planning by the teacher should include the following:

   a) Consideration for appropriate sequence between previous classroom situations and any anticipated classroom experiences;

   b) Consideration of means to care more adequately for individual and group needs;

   c) Consideration of ways to secure improvement in the response to pupils when planning;

   d) Selection of certain materials and references;

   e) Examination of any problems or difficulties that may be encountered by the students;

   f) Selection of content that may evoke new interests;

   g) Consideration of useful procedures to motivate thinking and discussion by the students. (Robert S. Harnack, Pupil-Teacher Planning, unpublished)
   Teachers must be well prepared in subject matter

and grade level understandings. Without in-depth academic background and a reservoir of activity-related ideas, the teacher cannot hope to have the confidence needed to guide others in skillful planning.

Before approaching the class with this stage of pupil-teacher planning, the teacher should have established a tentative outline for the unit of study, including all the necessary phases. Should the school system dictate subject topics to be taught, adaptations for specific class needs can be developed with the students.

5. Goals should be established relating to the topic of study.

By having a supply of ideas in mind, the teacher should guide students in establishing limits of study. One of the initial questions to put before the class should be: Why should we be studying this topic? If students have put some thought into the purposes for their work, the work will take on greater importance and it will help in making wise choices of activities.

6. Topics can be broken down into smaller areas of study.

It is important that each student locates an area in which he can work successfully. If students create an individual problem to be solved instead of concentrating efforts on a general topic, the knowledge and understandings gained become more meaningful. A key question to stimulate identification of individual areas of study could be: What do we need to know in order to solve our main problem? Sometimes a field trip or a general information-finding session can clear the way for answers to this question.

7. Teacher provides guidance in determination of specific responsibilities to be filled.

A key question to use is: How can we solve our problem? It is important that each student become aware of his specific responsibilities and how they fit into the overall picture. Outlining guidelines with the students will help. Considerations such as necessity for cooperation, utilization of available resources, suggestions for profitable activities and delineation of responsibilities are important ones to make.

It is important to emphasize here that other-than planning activities be interspersed among the planning phases so that students don't get bogged down in the planning itself.

8. Teacher insures that students understand how to work in small groups.

Directions for working in small groups must be explicit. Specific guidelines must be set so that each member of the group understands his role. The teacher must circulate among the groups to provide appropriate guidance. Emphasis must be put on leadership and followership principles, ultimately resulting in the responsible solution of a common problem.

9. Teacher should provide expert guidance in developing students' ability to do research work.

Research is a complex and difficult task to perform. This skill must be taught in detailed steps. Ample practice must be provided to insure that students achieve success at their own rates of speed. Remember that reading, writing, outlining and the scientific process are involved in good research. Be sure students are thoroughly prepared in these aspects.

10. Students should be involved in establishing reasonable time limits.

A sequential schedule of events should be planned. The organization of such should emphasize that each student's contribution must be completed by a certain time so that others may not be inconvenienced in fulfilling their related responsibilities. A tentative date should be set for pulling together related materials for evaluation and/or presentation.

11. Flexible facilities are more conducive to project-planning activities.

This point merely emphasizes the classroom flexibility required of group work. Chairs and other furniture must be movable; students must be provided opportunities to use other rooms and facilities if needed.

12. Students should be involved in securing instructional resources, materials and supplies needed for work.

The teacher should have lists of books, instructional materials and such at his fingertips for ready reference. Students can then be guided to find resources for research, materials for construction, and names of persons who might serve as valuable human resources. Student utilization of audio-visual equipment and materials by individuals and groups can prove helpful.

13. There must be opportunities for continuous planning.

It must be emphasized that students need continuous guidance in planning if objectives of both the unit and of pupil-teacher planning are to be fulfilled. Keep in mind the point of the unit: that students are trying to solve an important problem in order to arrive at a needed solution. Individualized responsibilities in terms of abilities can be strengthened by guiding more capable students into assuming additional challenges in meeting problems. Those of lesser ability can be encouraged through close guidance.

14. There should be opportunities for continuous evaluation.

Basically, evaluation begins as soon as planning begins. By asking where we are going, how we are doing and how we can do better, evaluation can take place daily with individuals, small groups or the whole class. This technique can serve to keep the teacher apprised of the situation and helps organize the work of the class. Moreover, the teacher can be supportive in a guided discovery process.

Other kinds of evaluation can involve class discussion, panel discussions, peer evaluation, self evaluation, written evaluation, observation, quizzes and tests, weekly logs and display of individual and group projects. Planning and evaluation work hand-in-hand to broaden fields of understanding and to supply meaningful evidence relating to fulfillment of objectives.

15. Students should synthesize and analyze knowledge and understandings gained from pupil-teacher planning and the unit.

Students should be helped to visualize the relationship of their own work to the total project. The solution of the problems in the total framework should be clearly understood. The results of pupil-teacher planning should be synthesized and analyzed so that an appreciation and understanding of its use can be gained.

The foregoing criteria for teacher-pupil planning represent a technique, a methodology if you will, which has been utilized by democratically-oriented teachers for many years. One can plainly see that its thrust is toward individualization of instruction with respect granted for the worth of each individual. What could be of greater value in teaching-learning relationships?

Selected Bibliography

Beauchamp, George A. *Planning The Elementary School Curriculum*. New York: Allyn & Bacon, 1956.

Burton, William H. *The Guidance of Learning Activities*. 3rd ed. New York: Appleton-Century-Crofts, 1962.

Bush, Robert H. *The Teacher-Pupil Relationship*. Englewood Cliffs, N.J.: Prentice-Hall, 1954.

Harnack, Robert S. *Pupil-Teacher Planning*. (Unpublished)

Harnack, Robert S. *The Teacher: Decision Maker and Curriculum Planner*. Scranton, PA: International Textbook Co., 1968.

Horace Mann—Lincoln Institute of School Experimentation. *The Teacher's Role in Pupil Teacher Planning*. New York: Bureau of Publications, Teachers' College, Columbia University, 1947.

Lee, J. Murray and Davis M. *The Child and His Curriculum*. 3rd ed. New York: Appleton-Century-Crofts, 1960.

Miel, Alice et al. *Cooperative Procedures in Learning*. New York: Bureau of Publications, Teachers' College, Columbia University, 1952.

THE AUTHOR PRESENTS, IN THE FOLLOWING AR-
TICLE, THE INSTRUCTIONAL DEVELOPMENT SYSTEM.
THIS SYSTEM, IN WHICH THE PUPIL IS CENTRAL,
APPLIES TO BOTH THE FORMAL SCHOOL SETTING
AND INFORMAL LEARNING OUTSIDE THE SCHOOL.
SEVERAL MODELS ARE INCLUDED THAT DELINEATE
HOW PUPILS CAN MAKE DECISIONS ABOUT THEIR
LEARNING.

INSTRUCTIONAL DEVELOPMENT
FROM THE LEARNER'S POINT OF VIEW

Paul A. Scholl

*Reprinted from Audiovisual Instruction, Vol. 17,
No. 1 (January 1972), pp. 18-20, by permission
of the Association for Educational Communications and Technology.*

Much of the information about Instructional Development is written from the point of view of the designer or
system manager. Generally the concern is for breaking down
the design task into its component parts—task analysis, writing behavior objectives, designing instructional activities,
specifying sequence, evaluating results, etc.

All this tends to make the student an afterthought in
the process. Since it is for the student that all the development, instruction and evaluation is undertaken, he should be
central to the total process. Instructional developers, managers, teachers, curriculum developers, etc. might well take
one step back and analyze the informal everyday process of
human learning.

When learning is described as a linear process exempli-
fied by "school" (See Figure 1), the student starts with a

45

task, is given a way-to-learn, is subjected to the learning experience, and is evaluated by the school system. For most of us, this model is quite inadequate if we look at the process either as the student we have been or as the teacher we hope we are.

Figure 2 presents a systems model for learning. This model can be applied to both informal learning outside the school and the learning which should take place in the school. The student enters the system by accepting a task. This task can be specified by the institution, or it may be self-generated by the student. In all cases it must be accepted by the learner as a task he wants to undertake or as an objective he will work to achieve. At this point the learner evaluates the task and himself. In some cases the student may be able to do the task because of previous learning experiences. In other cases he may decide he needs more training, or that he knows absolutely nothing about the subject, or that he cannot perform the skill at all. He will, in the latter case, consider various ways to learn which may help him reach his goal. Double arrows between ways to learn and learner evaluation indicate a complex interaction where the student considers the various ways to learn in relation to the task and his own personal predisposition to undertake certain learning tasks as a whole.

When the student accepts a way to learn, he has essentially decided to undertake an experience. This experience could be interaction with a teacher, interaction with media, or any one of a long list of learning tasks. The student's problem at this point of his learning cycle is to make the best use of his time and the most efficient use of the chosen way to learn. The student must have access to the men, materials and/or machines in the best combinations. He might well ask to be guided by a tutor to be able to use the best resources in the best ways.

At any time during the experience with a way to learn, the learner can evaluate the experience and choose another way to learn if the first choice proves to be a poor one. At any time during the cycle of self-evaluation, possible ways to learn, and experience the learner may exit from the process. He may feel he has learned the task well enough to use his knowledge or skill in a real life setting. And this is what it's all about.

As indicated in Figure 3, if a system evaluation or a criterion test is added to the learning model, a feedback loop to the task completes the self-correcting factor which is a vital part of all systems.

Note that the system is totally dependent upon the action of the individual. If the individual enters the system and cannot find a task which he is willing to accept, he can exit. If the learner evaluates the ways to learn and arrives at a negative evaluation, he may exit. The system will ultimately take note of these exits and will adjust the task required or size of step to one that is reasonable by the learner's standards.

It should be noted that the learning tasks can be as large or as small as a particular area, subject matter, or skill may require. A task may be considered something as small as learning to balance a checkbook or something as complex as learning to be a tool and die maker.

The system gives no reward-by-certification to the learner. System evaluation is a criterion which the learner meets at some point in time. The ultimate criterion of this system is whether or not a student can perform the learned skills satisfactorily in a life situation. After all, the ultimate goal for someone who wants to learn to scuba dive is to use scuba equipment for his pleasure and/or profit in such a way that he does not endanger his own life or the lives of others. This does not necessarily mean that he need be an expert, but at the least he must know his competencies and limitations.

A learner controlling his own curriculum may not be acceptable to those who feel a "well-rounded education" is necessary for the "complete man." The emphasis proposed here does give a vocational slant to education. However, as a learner and human being, I would like to learn to appreciate literature, music, art, and the dance at a time and place of my own choosing, by exposing myself to the experiences I choose.

The emphasis of this article on learning assumes an open-entry system of learning. A learner should not be denied the opportunity to seek out or engage in any learning exper-

Figure 1

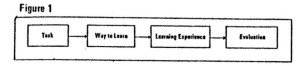

Figure 2

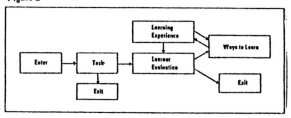

Figure 3

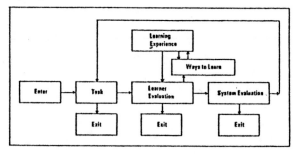

48

ience which meets his needs.

The system does have a negative feature. It allows students to fail. On the other hand, it requires no certification to enter. It does not make the graduation from grammar school a necessary prerequisite to the entry into or the acceptance of high school tasks.

A system based on the concept of learning proposed here has the potential to be of great practical value in the everyday world as expressed by our social, political and institutionalized educational system. One value is that it spotlights at least one significant question which is not usually asked in discussions of Instructional Development.

After an Instructional Development meeting at the 1971 AECT Convention, a small group was reacting to the presentation. One person found it frightening to think we already have some individuals who have the title "Instructional Developer," and this person has, or will have, the power to specify a task, write behavioral objectives, control the instructional tasks, and the sequence in which students will receive the tasks. The question is, who shall be given the right to decide these basic issues?

I submit that the student should be given the absolute right to decide his own way to learn and his own learning sequence. Accepting this statement, the Instructional Developer has a mandate to provide as many ways to learn as possible and the student has the responsibility to make the effort to learn.

THE NEXT ARTICLE MAINTAINS THAT PUPILS CAN
AND MUST BE INVOLVED IN CURRICULUM DEVELOP-
MENT. MARQUIS SUGGESTS THAT THREE BASIC
PREMISES UNDERLIE THE INCLUSION OF PUPILS IN
CURRICULUM MATTERS. ALSO, INCLUDED IN THE
ARTICLE, IS A DISCUSSION CONCERNING THE SPE-
CIFIC NATURE AND EFFECTS OF PUPIL INVOLVE-
MENT IN DESIGNING THE CURRICULUM.

CURRICULUM DEVELOPMENT:
CAN STUDENTS BE INVOLVED?

Romeo Marquis

*Reprinted from NASSP Bulletin, Vol. LVII, No.
373 (May 1973), pp. 127-131, by permission of
the National Association of Secondary School
Principals.*

The matter of student involvement in school affairs
is an issue which has been debated for a long time. Where
student involvement does exist, it is often restricted to coordination of student smoking areas, operation of student
lounges, participation on activities committees, and the like.
While these functions are important, they do not provide for
direct involvement by students in the affairs of formal instruction. Direct student involvement in matters of curriculum must be instituted in schools where it is non-existent
and it probably should be expanded in most schools where
it already exists.

Preliminary Considerations

The principal who wishes to consider student involve-

51

ment in curriculum matters must first come to grips with three basic premises. His own reactions to these will determine in large part the manner in which he can tap the reservoir of student awareness at his disposal.

Premise No. 1: Curriculum development is not an exclusive function of teachers and administrators.

Premise No. 2: High school students are relatively well versed in curriculum matters.

Premise No. 3: Student involvement in curriculum development does not mean that students will eventually dictate what is to be taught and how.

Reactions to these premises ought to be developed in a systematic and logical manner so as to void the pitfalls of reasoning from emotion. Too often we seek solutions that only seem to solve our problems and are based on ease, comfort, and non-controversiality. The most systematic approach to reacting to these premises rests in reasonable logic tied to a solid factual base. Full development of these premises would require much more space than is available here, so for the purposes of this article, I'm simply going to assume that you will accept them based on your own philosophy of education and the outer limits that I will now establish.

The curriculum design is influenced by factors outside the realm of education per se is generally accepted as fact. These outside influences come from homes, churches, social agencies, politics, textbook companies, industry, and many many other sources. Many of these same influences come to bear on the minds of our students, making them much more aware of curriculum matters than they have ever been. To say that students are instructional technologists in a literal sense would probably not stand the tests of logic, but all of us have certainly heard and read about the effects of mass media on student awareness. Also, curriculum design and content are not items that are very well camouflaged, and to say that our own efforts have not caused pupils to be better informed in these areas would be a rather serious indictment of our own schools.

Finally, let's examine the theory that if they are given an inch, students will take a mile and, therefore, want to dictate what is to be taught and how. While there are always some exceptions, expansion of student involvement in non-curriculum areas simply has not led to mass takeovers of schools by kids. It must be understood, though, that student involvement is not a handout. It is a shared experience in which appropriate leadership must be exerted by teachers and administrators. On that basis there need not be any serious concern about "radical youths" telling teachers what to teach and how. On the basis of these arguments, we can draw the following conclusion:

If curriculum development is not an exclusive function of educators, and if students are relatively well versed in curriculum matters, and if student involvement does not mean that students will eventually dictate what is to be taught and how, then students must be given the opportunity to become more involved in curriculum development.

Some Working Examples

The next question would seek to logically establish the nature and effects of student involvement. In examining this broad area, I would like to draw from some of our experiences at Presque Isle High School. I certainly do not classify our approaches as unique, innovative, or especially imaginative—but they do seem to be working. As can be expected, the opinions of our faculty members are not homogeneous, but the differences in thinking seem to stem from the degree of involvement rather than from the question of to-involve-or-not-to-involve.

Student involvement in curriculum design in our school is taking on a rather diverse character, consisting of classroom involvement, committee involvement, and large-scale involvement. I must admit that such involvement in our school had a very limited (almost non-existent) foundation in committee and large-scale involvement until the fall of 1971; however, student involvement in classroom planning has been functional for some time because of the efforts of some perceptive and forward-thinking teachers. For them, expansion of opportunities for student involvement is but another step in the right direction.

Student involvement on ad hoc committees is generating some rather interesting results in curriculum and curriculum-related areas. Our first real attempt at staff-student involvement was in committee work on a study hall committee. Seven students and eight staff members participated. The purpose of the committee was to develop a list of appropriate ideas for student use on unassigned time.

In the area of final exams, our student council proposed a very significant change in the policy for seniors. Although the scope of the proposal is not directly related to this presentation, the involvement of the student council as a curriculum committee is. The council sought and received ideas from faculty members, administrators, and board members, and presented a final proposal that was well prepared. Educationally sound, it was favorably received by most of the school community and was adopted last May.

Student involvement of a slightly different nature is also being established through a network of school community councils. There will be four such councils. The council on inter-staff relations will deal with communications, staff roles, and staff structure; the council on the school community concept will deal with general school atmosphere, teacher-pupil relationships, and school government; the council on instructional technology will deal with instructional planning, classroom processes, and other areas of curriculum design; the council on learning assessment will deal with the effects of the school on students, in both the cognitive and affective domains. Student involvement is vital to the success of these councils, and such involvement should provide appropriate student input into the real functions of learning.

Aside from short as well as exhaustive surveys of student opinion, our next effort at large-scale student involvement in curriculum development will take place when we begin to register students for next year. Our program of studies lists almost 200 different courses and programs. These include a wide variety of semester courses and out-of-school experiences. But the clincher comes when the student will be asked to suggest a unique program for himself if he feels that our listed programs do not fit his particular learning interests, abilities, and styles. I honestly don't know what the results will be. We may get very few suggestions, yet the number of special requests might surprise us. At any rate, the results will undoubtedly be interesting and meaningful.

Summary and Implications

Representative involvement in our school will soon include some 75-100 students. Large-scale involvement, of course, gives every student the opportunity to participate. The entire function of curriculum development can be compared to a matching game, although the seriousness of this particular game is such that the success of the school community depends upon it. The matching game in which the principal must be the catalyst deals with the casting of special combintions which establish the best possible learning atmosphere for pupils. The ingredients of these learning atmospheres are students and their learning styles, teachers and their teaching styles, curriculum content, materials, and resources. The basic premise of this presentation is that students should be heavily involved in the casting of these combinations.

Rapidly increasing complexity of curriculum development and a host of other factors have just about wiped out the day of unilateral decision making by principals. Although optimum involvement by all members of the school community may bring certain pressures to bear on the high school principal, such involvement constitutes an extremely valuable resource for him and serves to broaden his base of maneuverability and decision making. A vital part of that broad base is student involvement in matters of formal instruction. It is good that students can be involved in coordination of non-curriculum matters, but it is not enough.

Most students have the competence and the right to make significant decisions concerning their own learning if they are provided appropriate leadership, and high school principals must assume responsibility for initiating that leadership and ensuring its continuity. Only then will students truly appreciate the piece of the action that is rightfully theirs; and only then will students, teachers, and administrators be able to exert a truly unified effort as they strive to reach common goals.

IN THE FOLLOWING ARTICLE, THE AUTHORS DIS-
CUSS COOPERATIVE TEACHER-STUDENT PLANNING
IN THE AREAS OF PEER TEACHING AND STUDENT
MOTIVATED SELF-INSTRUCTION. THESE LEARNING
ENVIRONMENTS REQUIRE CREATIVITY, IMAGINA-
TION, INVOLVEMENT AND LEADERSHIP ON THE
PART OF STUDENTS. STEP-BY-STEP COOPERATIVE
PLANNING APPROACHES ARE PRESENTED FOR THE
PEER TEACHING INSTRUCTIONAL DESIGN MODEL
AND THE SELF-INSTRUCTION INSTRUCTIONAL DE-
SIGN MODEL.

TEACHER-STUDENT COOPERATIVE INSTRUCTIONAL DESIGN MODELS FOR PEER TEACHING AND STUDENT MOTIVATED SELF-INSTRUCTION

David M. Moore and Ruth D. Harris

Reprinted with permission from Educational Technology, Vol. 16, No. 4 (April 1976), pp. 21-24. "Copyright © 1976 by Educational Technology Publications, Inc."

The premise of this article is that instructional design can be used effectively in cooperative planning of instruction with students, primarily in the areas of peer teaching and student motivated self-instruction. Student motivated self-instruction, as used in this article, refers mainly to student initiated projects; e.g., contractual learning.

Cooperative planning is not intended to make teachers give up their responsibilities or authority in lesson planning; it is intended, however, to allow teachers and students to work cooperatively in areas where the students have special skills and interests that would benefit the entire class or individual students.

Self-instruction can be defined as self-contained, self-paced activity toward a stated objective using the approach most interesting to the student. Peer teaching involves one student teaching another student or group of students. The authors are interested in both of these types of student involvement activities and in the way in which learning activity can be logically planned and presented. Both types of student activity have several things in common, notably that they require student involvement and initiative.

The Peer Teaching Instructional Design Model*

Teacher-pupil cooperative planning is not a haphazard affair. In order to make the outcome productive, a logical, step-by-step approach is needed. Basically this approach involves (1) determination of student needs, statements of intended outcomes and development of content; (2) selection of a teaching technique or strategy and the appropriate media and resources; (3) the presentation itself; and (4) evaluation of the process. Cooperative planning must be sequential and involve both the teacher and the student, or a group of students.

In any type of cooperative activity between teacher and pupil, the skills, competencies and experiences of both the teacher and the student should be utilized. The teacher obviously has had training in lesson planning and presentation. Assistance should be given to the student in planning the learning experience. With cooperative instructional development in peer teaching, the key role of the teacher is as a facilitator of learning. The teacher must maximize the likelihood that the student will be fully engaged in a productive learning activity. Teachers will be compelled to make provisions for involvement rather than passive exploration of the topic in question. Figure 1 illustrates how the following steps interrelate with each other.

---

*This model has been modified and adapted from an earlier model developed by the authors which appeared in the *Journal of Home Economics*, January 1975.

FIGURE 1

The Peer Teaching Instructional Design Model

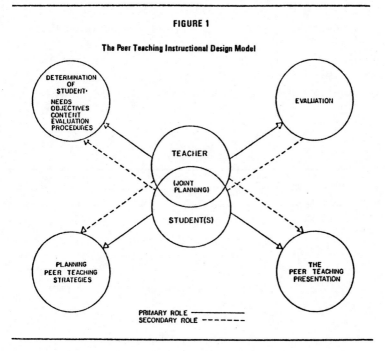

Determination of Needs, Objectives, Content and Evaluation Procedures

The teacher's role is important in the area of establishing needs, setting behavioral objectives and determining content. The teacher should make sure that the goals and objectives of the lesson are seriously considered and understood by the peer teacher. The student can also play an important role in these areas and should provide suggestions. The criteria for the evaluation will be determined by the student and the teacher.

Evaluation and reevaluation of the presentation, its content and the original objectives will fall within the teacher's prime responsibility. The student presenters as well as other class members should be asked for their input and recommendations. Time should be set aside in order that the student presenters and the teacher, on a one-to-one basis, can discuss all aspects of the presentation. If in the presentation the student offered misinformation or concepts which might be misinterpreted, the teacher should point these out to the student and offer him time in class to make corrections.

The Self-Instruction Instructional Design Model

Teachers who wish to individualize instruction or allow students to contract learning segments can involve basically the same approach as the model in Figure 1, with a few minor changes. Student motivated self-instruction, as the name implies, is more personal; the student is working on his own primarily because of his own interest. Seldom would there be a student presentation, as in peer teaching. The activity when completed would be discussed in an individual session between the student and teacher. A logical approach should be taken in planning this activity. Figure 2 depicts such an approach to instructional design.

Determination of Needs, Objectives, Content and Evaluation Procedures

As in the first model, the teacher and student work together in determining the needs, objectives and content.

FIGURE 2

The Self-Instruction Instructional Design Model

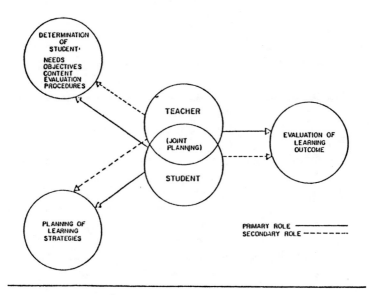

However, in this model, the student plays the primary role; e.g., the needs and objectives are developed primarily by the student, with assistance from the teacher. The needs and objectives should be formulated by the student in line with his interests and concerns. However, like the earlier model, evaluation procedures and criteria should be developed at this time. This would also be the time, if the teacher or student want a contract, that such an agreement is made.

The teacher serves as a resource person from whom the student can find sources of information or possible ways to attack the learning problem. It is the student's responsibility to determine the exact learning strategy, time frame and the form the final products will take.

In evaluating the process, the teacher and student become equals, with each helping and evaluating the final product based on the predetermined procedures.

Summary

We do not advocate that all instruction or classroom presentations be planned and presented using cooperative teacher-student planning. But in areas where students have the interests and/or can make a vital contribution, cooperative planning is recommended.

The Peer Teaching Instructional Design Model may be used with students at all grade levels in small groups or large groups. The Self-Instruction Instructional Design Model is recommended for student initiated learning projects.

If, at the evaluation stage of either model, the teacher and student agree that the objectives, content and interest level would be suitable, the process might be recycled into the other model. For example, after a student presentation to a group, the student might decide that he or she would like to delve into the subject more intensely. The process of the self-instructional model may be used, or vice-versa.

In these learning environments, the student is encouraged to develop leadership skills and exhibit creativity in the classroom.

THE NEXT ARTICLE DESCRIBES PUPIL-TEACHER DE-
CISION MAKING IN THE ELEMENTARY CLASSROOM.
VARIOUS DECISION MAKING SKILLS ARE PRESENTED
FOR ENABLING PUPILS TO DEAL WITH REAL LIFE
PROBLEM-SOLVING SITUATIONS. THE ARTICLE ALSO
SETS FORTH GUIDELINES FOR MOTIVATING AND
GUIDING PUPIL-TEACHER DECISION MAKING.

HOW TO SUCCESSFULLY INVOLVE ELEMENTARY
SCHOOL PUPILS IN CLASSROOM DECISION MAKING

William J. Stewart

*Reprinted with permission from Peabody Journal
of Education, Vol. 54, No. 2 (January 1977),
pp. 117-119. Copyright 1977 by George Peabody
College of Vanderbilt University.*

Are elementary school teachers making many classroom decisions that pupils can help to decide? Do teachers
always consider and best use children's suggestions? In what
ways can teachers create more opportunities for pupils to
develop and to use decision making skills? How can teachers
best relate pupils' decision making to actual life experiences?
In this article, I intend to explain the pupil-teacher planning
concept in light of these important questions.

The teacher who simply sets aside a specific time
period to teach decision-making skills does not enable pupils
to learn to choose as a part of the normal, ongoing experience of living. When children are allowed to make decisions
only within narrowly defined limits, it becomes exceedingly
difficult, if not impossible, for them to perceive how they
can solve their everyday problems through the decision making process.

63

The following episode occurred in a kindergarten class:

The children were sitting in chairs arranged in a circle. Delays had occurred when Debbie had to tell Miss Jarvis about her birthday party next Sunday. Arnie wanted to know if it was his turn to water the plants, and Mary had just presented Miss Jarvis with some brightly colored ribbons. Then, Miss Jarvis stood at the chalkboard and printed a schedule for the day's activities, as the class made suggestions about what they should do first, then next. No serious disagreements arose over the plans, but Susan and Cynthia criticized Tony at one point for not putting the paint brushes away during cleanup time yesterday. Miss Jarvis asked Tony if he would like to show everybody he could put away the paint brushes by assuming this responsibility today. Fifteen children offered suggestions about activities, and a frequent showing of hands indicated consensus. Clearly, not only everybody had a housekeeping or leadership role, but everybody in the class wanted his turn at various roles.

Obviously, this kindergarten class demonstrated an ability to think together, to formulate plans. to assess strengths and weaknesses, to reach decisions acceptable to the entire class. Thus, Miss Jarvis used pupil-teacher planning to help the class to relate its everyday experiences, concerns, and problems to making decisions, to carrying them out, and to evaluating results.

Decision-Oriented Skills

Since pupil-teacher planning can work in the kindergarten, pupils' opportunities for making decisions, through shared planning, should become more frequent and sophisticated with each succeeding grade level. Moreover, teachers should continually strive to provide necessary help, guidance, and support for fostering the development and refinement of decision making skills.

Elementary teachers, by involving pupils in a wide variety of life centered problem-solving situations, can effectively nurture each child's appreciation, knowledge, and understanding concerning cooperative decision making. As the teacher begins to think about using pupil-teacher planning to provide children with real life problem-solving opportunities, he/she should consider the following decision-oriented skills:

Basic Skills. What life-centered decision making opportunities, as evolved through pupil-teacher planning, can the pupils have regarding such basic skills as following printed directions, listening with discrimination, organizing ideas and computation?

Expressional Skills. In how many ways can the pupil be helped, through pupil-teacher planning, to render decisions concerning expression of their emotions and feelings? Starting with everyday experiences, children can help in making decisions related to such expressional modes as dancing, speaking, and writing.

Exploratory Skills. How can pupil-teacher planning stimulate decision making concerning what pupils see, hear, and touch in their everyday living? Are there plants and animals to care for? What things can they assemble and disassemble? Have the children explored every part of the school—inside and out? How can they explore their community?

Thinking Skills. How can pupil-teacher planning help pupils to think about their everyday curiosities? For example, children frequently ask such questions as what makes it rain, why is the sky blue, and why is the ocean salty?

Guidelines for Cooperative Planning

Pupil-teacher planning can combine meaningful teaching and purposeful learning to provide the pupils with innumerable opportunities to participate in classroom decision making. The degree, however, to which shared planning manifests itself in the form of actual pupil-teacher decisions

65

directly relates to how well the teacher considers and employs the pupil-teacher planning concept.

The remainder of this article presents and discusses guidelines for using pupil-teacher planning to motivate and to guide cooperative decision making. Eight guidelines are discussed in the following paragraphs. I do not claim that these eight represent all that one needs for shared classroom decision making.

1. Necessarily, the teacher must preplan thoroughly to lay the groundwork for pupil-teacher planning. Pupil-teacher planning, preceded by careful preliminary preparation, better enables the teacher to adjust the curriculum plan to pupils' interests and needs.

2. The teacher should exert a significant effort to involve each pupil as fully as possible under the circumstances. Every pupil should be motivated to contribute to the thinking, planning, and decision making of the total group.

3. The teacher should encourage pupils to assess their suggested ideas and to improve their ability to predict possible outcomes. More than likely, pupils will contribute many suggestions. The children, however, should be encouraged to assess their suggestions to determine appropriateness, to discover relationships, to eliminate overlap and to determine if they can arrange their ideas into logical and sequential order.

4. Attention should focus on both the pupils' expressed needs and the teacher's specific requirements and recommendations. A balance always must be struck between the pupils' expressed needs and the teacher's conception of what each pupil needs.

5. Pupil-teacher planning, to be fully effective, must be perceived by teachers and pupils as important, meaningful, and necessary. Pupil-teacher planning should not be regarded as the easy way out. Shared planning, rather,

requires a plain old roll-up-your-sleeves kind of effort and dedication.

6.   The teacher's ideas and plans should never be imposed against the will of the group. Teachers, even though they should devise preliminary plans, should not expect the group to automatically accept their suggestions.

7.   The affective domain, as well as the cognitive domain, should be included in pupil-teacher planning efforts. The teacher should always attempt to build pupil-teacher planning activities on decision making for total living, instead of just on content and skill acquisition.

8.   Pupil-teacher planning should be regarded as a flexible process easily modified to accommodate a wide variety of educational demands and situations. When teachers possess clear knowledge and understanding of cooperative planning, then the possibilities concerning the how, when, and where to carry on shared planning are necessarily extremely extensive and divergent.

Elementary school curriculum leaders should continually watch for ways to encourage, help and support those teachers interested in pupil-teacher planning. To this end, every effort should be exerted to provide staff training for those teachers desiring to study and to use cooperative classroom decision making. Only through professional growth activities can pupil-teacher planning work effectively.

In summary, cooperative classroom planning constitutes an important instructional method because its basic purpose emphasizes and promotes participatory decision making — a fundamental democratic principle. Meaningful learning can occur through shared planning activities since pupils are able to formulate decisions — both individually and collectively — about lifelike concerns, interests and problems. Essentially, cooperative classroom planning can provide the pupils with many opportunities to learn how to plan together; to learn how to make decisions together; to learn how to evaluate experiences together and to learn how to get along with each other.

THE FOLLOWING ARTICLE EXAMINES A PILOT
COURSE IN COMPUTER PROGRAMMING FOR SIXTH
GRADE PUPILS. THE PUPILS WERE INVOLVED IN
WRITING THEIR OWN COMPUTER PROGRAMS. THE
COMPUTER WAS APPLIED TO INTRODUCE NEW CON-
CEPTS TO PUPILS, AND TO DETERMINE THE PUPILS.
PROBLEM-SOLVING TECHNIQUES AND LEARNING
PROCESSES.

DEVELOPING COMPUTER LITERACY IN CHILDREN: SOME OBSERVATIONS AND SUGGESTIONS

Thomas G. Holzman and Robert Glaser

*Reprinted with permission from Educational
Technology, Vol. 17, No. 8 (August 1977), pp.
5-11. "Copyright © 1977 by Educational Technology Publications, Inc."*

With recent developments in technology, computers
have become increasingly accessible to a growing number of
people. Time-sharing systems have facilitated the use of computers for educational purposes, and Computer-Assisted Instruction (CAI) is now a reality in a number of elementary
schools. To date, CAI has been predominantly used as a
means for providing students with drill and practice in a
variety of academic subject areas. However, other potential
uses of the computer for educational purposes are being explored. One of these is the possibility of young children
learning to write their own computer programs. The acquisition of computer programming skills might well serve as a
medium in which new concepts (particularly in mathematics
and logic) can be introduced to young students in a way that
captures their interest and enables them to readily find appli-

cations for those concepts. Likewise, by studying the kinds of programs the children write and the types of programming concepts with which they experience difficulty, some interesting facts might be acquired about children's problem-solving techniques and learning processes.

Previous attempts to teach programming skills to pre-college students have produced encouraging results. Feurzeig, Grant, Lukas and Lukas (1971) have found that the LOGO computer language can be a useful medium for conveying concepts in mathematics and logic. Dwyer's (1974, 1975) high school students have developed programs in the BASIC language for computer-assisted music synthesizers, computer-controlled flight simulators and computer-operated robots, to name a few. The present study combined some of the features of these past projects into a curriculum specifically directed toward pre-adolescent children.

Two computer programming languages, LOGO and FOCAL, were selected for study. These languages share a number of features between themselves and with other, widely used languages, such as BASIC. Consequently, whether a student was instructed in LOGO or FOCAL, the principal concepts would be generalizable to other computer languages and would thus permit the student to use his knowledge of computers in a wide variety of contexts. At the same time, FOCAL and LOGO have certain distinct capabilities and requirements: LOGO is better suited to operate on text (e.g., joining syllables into words and recognizing names), while FOCAL permits a wider range of mathematical applications. One aim of this project was to determine which parts of these different languages seemed best suited to the needs and abilities of 11-year-old children.

Facilities
Computer Laboratory
Six children, from the sixth grade of a local school, were selected by their teacher to participate in the computer curriculum. Computer terminals at the University of Pittsburgh's Learning Research and Development Center were made available to the student programmers. Each child worked at a separate terminal for one or two one-hour

sessions per week over a period of about six months. In addition to the conventional computer terminals, students of the LOGO computer language were provided with a remote control device known as the "turtle". The turtle is a mechanical, hemisphere-shaped vehicle on wheels, a little more than a foot in diameter. It is connected by a long electrical cord to a computer terminal, from which it is programmed. Special LOGO commands make the turtle go forward, backward, right and left. Attached to the bottom of the turtle is a ballpoint pen which can be raised or lowered on command from the terminal. This permits computer programs that direct the turtle to write or draw as it moves over its paper-covered platform.

Computer Manuals

Three of the six students were assigned on LOGO, and the other three learned FOCAL. The first author served as the teacher for both groups of children, although most of the teaching was provided through a self-instructional manual for each language. The manual used for the LOGO students was adapted from one written by Roman and Heller (1974); the FOCAL manual was written by the children's teacher. Both manuals consisted of sets of booklets, each booklet providing information and suggesting programming exercises on a new command or some other feature of the language.

For the most part, the booklets were arranged in order of increasing difficulty with later taught skills building upon earlier ones. For instance, the students were taught how to make the computer print lines of the text. Then they were taught how to assemble individual lines of text into stories. Still later, they were taught how to combine these text-printing capabilities of the computer with its ability to evaluate mathematical expressions. In these programs, the computer typed out arithmetic problems, asked the user for his answer, and then compared the user's answer with the solution obtained when the computer evaluated the expression.

Instructional Outcomes

The students proceeded through their manuals without major difficulties in understanding the concepts that were presented. In fact, the only real obstacle to their progress was their relative lack of familiarity with the keyboards of their terminals. Some of the students had previously received typing lessons, and this significantly increased the rate at which they completed their programming assignments.

Students of both languages were introduced to such logical-mathematical and programming notions as conditionals, variables, random numbers and recursion of subroutines. In addition, FOCAL students had their first encounters with decimal points, exponentiation and the concepts of integers and absolute values. In the context of writing programs, the children learned some general techniques employed by expert problem-solvers in situations both inside and outside the domain of computer programming. For instance, the children were taught how to divide complex tasks or problems into simpler ones and how to assemble the results of these simple procedures into programs that met the demands of the complex task. In addition, the students developed trouble-shooting skills by using the computer's error messages and other outputs to isolate and correct mistakes in their programs.

Both the observations of the students' teacher and the comments of the students themselves and their parents indicated that the children very much enjoyed their encounters with the computer. The children especially liked composing recursive procedures which caused the computer to repeatedly type the same lines. Such procedures required only a few elementary programming steps and yet produced an enormous amount of printed output. In addition, the children were fascinated by some of the last booklets of the manuals which introduced rather complex simulation and game-playing programs. What such game-playing programs seem to have in common with the recursive procedures that also captivated the children is a great deal of computer responsiveness. That is, the students very much enjoyed programs that caused large amounts of overt activity and permitted a great deal of user-computer interaction.

72

Further evidence of this was the children's fascination with LOGO's BELL command, which produces a ring or high-pitched tone at the terminal. The students included the BELL command in many of their programs. The bell would sound just before the user was to input some response to the computer or to signal some key outcome in a game-playing program.

Course Projects

Upon completion of the last booklets of the programming manuals, the students were asked to use as much of their computer knowledge as possible to write course project programs of their choice. These projects were suggested as means for providing the students with a comprehensive review and integration of their programming knowledge. The programming exercises suggested in the manuals were relatively limited in focus compared with these project programs. The former exercises usually concentrated on the application of only one or two newly instructed skills, while the projects were to incorporate almost all of the features of the language into a "super program" of special interest to the student.

As is frequently the case in most educational situations, the students required some guidance in discovering the range of applicability of their knowledge. At first, they experienced difficulty in conceiving of interesting projects that utilized a significant portion of their computer skills. To give the children a feel for the kinds of programs that could be written by individuals with their level of programming ability, the teacher discussed some uses of the computer that adult programmers find valuable (e.g., employing the computer to administer tests or teach lessons). In addition, the teacher exhibited some game-playing programs on the computer, and some other game-playing programs suggested by Spencer (1968) were discussed. After the students were acquainted with the general types of programs that could be written, they soon formulated ideas for course projects. Brief descriptions of six project programs follow.

CAI Arithmetic

Three students became interested in composing computer-assisted instruction programs. The children were told that other students could come to the computer laboratory and use these CAI programs to help them with their school work. One FOCAL student wrote a program that would drill the user on multiplication and division tables, correct his answer, and compute his test score. The program permitted the user to try division problems only after passing the multiplication test. If a test was not passed, the computer printed out the appropriate set of tables (multiplication or division) for the user to study before taking the test again.

CAI Vocabulary

Another FOCAL student wrote a program for computer-assisted instruction in vocabulary. The computer printed a word and then printed three sentences using that word. The user was to indicate to the computer which sentence properly used the word. The computer corrected the answer, printed the dictionary definition of the word after the user chose a sentence, and kept score. There were two levels to the vocabulary test, and the computer did not permit the user to try the second level until the first level was passed.

CAI History

The third CAI program was written in LOGO. It quizzed the user on the American Civil War. The computer corrected all the answers and gave the user his test score. The program provided questions at three levels of difficulty, and the user was permitted to pass to a harder level only after successfully completing the easier level.

Fortune-telling

One of the FOCAL students wrote a fortune-telling program. This program asked the user for his date of birth. Then an algorithm found in Spencer (1968) was programmed to tell the user the day of the week on which he was born.

74

Finally, the student added subroutines that output the sign of the Zodiac corresponding to the user's birthday and prognosticated the user's fortune for a month of his choice.

Dice Game

One of the LOGO students developed a dice game as his project. This program utilized the computer's random number generator to stimulate throws of two dice by printing two integers between 1 and 6. The player bet on whether the total of the two dice would be under 7, over 7, or exactly 7. The computer initially credited the player with $5 and kept a running total of the winnings. The game continued until the player quit or lost all his money.

Turtle Program

The sixth project was developed by a LOGO student. He used the computer-controlled turtle as an airplane simulator. The directions for the program were typed out at the terminal, telling the user to pretend that the turtle was an airplane and that he was its pilot. The user chose one of 15 cities as his destination. Then he was asked how many gallons of fuel his plane had and how many miles could be flown per gallon of fuel. Using this information, the computer directed the turtle to move as close to the designated city as it could in scale miles. If sufficient fuel had been allocated to reach the destination, the pilot was informed of this at the terminal, and the turtle drew a "V" for "victory" on its "runway", the paper-covered platform over which it moved. If the turtle was not given sufficient fuel to reach the selected city, it "tailspinned" by making a series of 360-degree turns. The computer asked the crashing pilot if he had any last words. If he did, he typed these into the computer. These last words were then included in a news bulletin typed out at the terminal to give the details of the crash.

Comparisons of the Programming Languages

Probably the single most important criterion for selecting a programming language for children is the extent to which its commands and functions use words to convey meanings similar to those associated with the words in conversational English. Both LOGO and FOCAL fulfill this criterion quite well. For example, the LOGO user can make the computer print the message HELLO if he first types PRINT and then types HELLO enclosed in quotation marks. If the FOCAL user wants to know what the product of 12 times 12 is, he can simply type TYPE 12 X 12, and the computer will respond with the answer (144).

The BASIC computer language shares with FOCAL and LOGO this quality of conversational-style programming commands. Although BASIC was not taught to the students in this study, the nature of its commands, in addition to its widespread availability on many computer systems, make it a potentially suitable language for children. Since these three programming languages vary in a number of ways, a comparison of their respective characteristics can provide some interesting information about the suitability of these languages for the children's needs and abilities.

Manipulation of Text

As indicated in Figure 1, all three languages make it easy to program the computer to type out the same letters, numbers, words, or other combinations of characters that the programmer types in. The children quickly mastered this skill and enjoyed making frequent use of it. They composed little stories for the computer to print, as well as using this feature in combination with more complex subroutines. For instance, the TYPE and PRINT commands were put to good use to make the computer type out directions about how to properly use the game-playing programs and to output the test questions in the CAI programs.

In addition, the LOGO language allowed the students to join together, break up, or rearrange lines of text. An example of this feature is contained in the REDUCE program suggested in the LOGO manual. This program allowed the user to input any word or number into the computer. Then, by means of the BUTLAST operator, the computer suc-

Comparisons of Programming Languages

Extended BASIC	FOCAL	LOGO
Printing and Spacing	**Printing and Spacing**	**Printing and Spacing**
PRINT makes the computer type the characters that follow in quotation marks. If an arithmetic problem follows PRINT, the computer gives the answer. PRINT with nothing following it causes a line feed.	*TYPE* makes the computer type the characters that follow in quotation marks. If an arithmetic problem follows TYPE, the computer gives the answer. TYPE followed by an exclamation point causes a line feed.	*PRINT* makes the computer type the characters that follow in quotation marks. If an arithmetic problem follows PRINT, the computer gives the answer. PRINT followed by a pair of quotation marks causes a line feed.
		Text Operators
		FIRST isolates the first character in a group of characters.
		LAST isolates the last character in a group of characters.
		BUTFIRST eliminates the first character in a group of characters.
		BUTLAST eliminates the last character in a group of characters.
		WORD(S) merges together the separate groups of characters that follow.
Variables	**Variables**	**Variables**
LET assigns a value to a variable.	*SET* assigns a value to a variable.	*MAKE* assigns a value to a variable.
INPUT allows a user to assign a value to a variable during the execution of the program. The computer pauses so the user can type in the value of his choice.	*ASK* allows a user to assign a value to a variable during the execution of the program. The computer pauses so the user can type in the value of his choice.	*MAKE* and *REQUEST* are used together to allow the user to assign a value to a variable during the execution of the program. The computer pauses so the user can type in the value of his choice.
Subscripted variables are permitted.	Subscripted variables are permitted.	No subscripted variables are allowed.
Numerical Outputs	**Numerical Outputs**	**Numerical Outputs**
Decimal points and scientific notation are used in the computer's numerical outputs.	Decimal points and scientific notation are used in the computer's numerical outputs.	All numerical outputs are in integer form.
Mathematical Operators and Functions	**Mathematical Operators and Functions**	**Mathematical Operators and Functions**
+ (addition) - (subtraction) * (multiplication) / (division)	+ (addition) - (subtraction) * (multiplication) / (division)	+ (addition) - (subtraction) * (multiplication) / (division with truncated remainder)
		DIV (division yielding quotient and integer remainder)
↑ (exponentiation) SQR (square root) ABS (absolute value) RND (generates a random number)	↑ (exponentiation) SQRT (square root) FABS (absolute value) FRAN (generates a random number)	*RANDOM* generates a random number.
Trigonometric functions	Trigonometric functions	
Logarithmic functions	Logarithmic functions	

cessively lopped off one character from the end of the input and printed the result. For instance, REDUCE "BALL" would produce the output below.

BALL
BAL
BA
B

Other LOGO programs were written to join separate groups of characters into a single group by using the WORD operator. For instance, a program was composed that permitted the user to join any two groups of letters by typing JOIN and then, in quotation marks, typing the groups of letters to be joined. If the user typed JOIN "FAT" "HER", the computer would type FATHER. Programs of this nature were of moderate interest to the sixth graders in this study. Because of their concrete nature, such programs would probably appeal even more to younger children.

Use of Variables

All three computer languages make use of variables so that a single program, or a single step within a program, can be used repeatedly to perform a given function on different input values. For instance, a program might be written to make the computer count from 1 to 100 and then stop. Rather than using a hundred different PRINT or TYPE commands, the programmer can tell the computer to set some variable, perhaps X, equal to 1 and then successively increment X by 1 and print the result until X equals 100. The student-programmers enjoyed writing such counting programs and also included counters as subroutines in more complex programs. For instance, the child who composed the CAI arithmetic program used a successively incremented variable to keep track of how many test problems were generated by the computer. When the value reached 25, the computer left the question-generating subroutine and gave the user his test score. Within the question-generating subroutine, variables were also used so that all the test problems could be developed from one general equation. Specifically, by programming the multiplication test questions in terms of variables (e.g., X * Y = —) and then directing the computer to substitute random numbers for those variables, the programmer could generate any number of questions he wished from this one general problem statement.

All three languages have the added advantage of allowing values to be assigned to variables during the actual run of the program. For instance, a program might be written to find the number of ounces that corresponds to some given number of gallons. The variable X might be used in the program to stand for the number of gallons present. The computer would begin executing the program by asking the user for the number of gallons and would then substitute this value for X. Since there are 64 ounces per gallon, the computer would then multiply X by 64 and output the answer for the user's inspection. This on-line assignment of values to variables was very popular with students of both FOCAL and LOGO. They wrote many programs which permitted a great deal of interaction between the user and the computer.

In addition to their numerical capabilities, both LOGO and BASIC permit the input of non-numeric characters as the values of variables. The children greatly enjoyed writing programs that make full use of this character string recognition capability. For instance, the student who developed the turtleplane project used this feature to ask the crashing pilot for his "last words." The words input by the user during the program run were assigned to a variable and were later output in a news bulletin describing the crash and the pilot's comments. When a new user ran the program, his last words were assigned to the variable and were later output in the bulletin without requiring any change in the program itself.

Mathematical Power

As shown in Figure 1, all three languages use a variety of arithmetic operators. However, the specific operators that are available differ from language to language, as do the formats of the answers that the computer prints out. In terms of output formats, one of the most serious shortcomings of LOGO for older programmers is one of its greatest strengths for younger ones. Specifically, although all three languages can direct the computer to output the quotient for a division problem, the manner in which this answer is expressed differs from language to language. LOGO outputs the answer in terms of a quotient with an integer remainder. This is the format most familiar to students prior to sixth or seventh grade. On the other hand, FOCAL and BASIC express the answer in decimal notation. The latter format becomes standard in junior high school. Therefore, the suitability of a language for mathematical applications is largely determined by the student's place in their mathematics curriculum.

With respect to the specific types of mathematical operators and functions available to the programmer, Figure 1 indicates that FOCAL and BASIC provide a much greater variety. Of course, a number of these functions, such as the trigonometric ones, generally are of little or no use to most elementary school students. However, things like the square root, the absolute value, and the exponent can be of interest to students in the upper grades. Such operators and functions were used extensively by the FOCAL students in this study. For instance, the students wrote a program that asked the user to guess what number between 1 and 10 the computer was "thinking of". The computer used its built-in random number generator to arrive at its number. To insure that the computer didn't "think" of a negative number, the program applied the absolute value function to the random number generated by the computer. The user's guess was then compared with the computer's number, and the user was informed of the accuracy of his answer.

In terms of mathematical power, FOCAL and BASIC have the added advantage of permitting subscripted variables. This enables the computer to keep track of what values have been substituted for variables in the program and permits the use of some complex mathematical procedures. In developing the CAI arithmetic program discussed previously, the utility of subscripted variables became apparent. When no restrictions were placed on the numbers randomly generated by the computer for the test problems, the computer would sometimes print out two identical problems in succession. To avoid this, the teacher showed the student-programmer how to use subscripted variables. After the computer generated a number to be substituted for the variable in the test problem, the computer would compare this value with the one substituted in the immediately preceding problem. If the two values were the same, the computer would refrain from printing that problem and instead would generate another random number, continuing until a new problem was composed.

Implications of Students' Programming Behaviors
Language Suitability and Grade Level

Based on the different requirements and properties of the languages that have been discussed, it seems that the language chosen and the concepts to be emphasized in a children's computer curriculum should depend on the educational level of the participating students. For the sixth graders in the current study, both LOGO and FOCAL seemed acceptable, because the children were at a transitional stage in their knowledge of mathematical concepts like decimal notation and square roots. Children a year or two younger, however, would probably benefit more from a language like LOGO. LOGO's answers to arithmetic problems always occur in the integer format familiar to young children. Furthermore, LOGO can initially catch the young child's interest by its many non-mathematical capabilities. For instance, words may be used as inputs to variables, so the computer can ask the user for his name, and then address him by name during the rest of the program run. Likewise, the LOGO programs which join letters into words and words into sentences should be particularly interesting for students in the early grades. Finally, the very concrete application of LOGO to direct the activities of the turtle makes it especially well suited to children since they can see physical outcomes of their mental efforts.

For adolescents and adults, FOCAL and BASIC seem more appropriate than LOGO. They contain certain arithmetic, trigonometric and logarithmic functions that can be valuable in solving the types of problems commonly encountered in high school and college mathematics and science courses. Also, because they permit the use of subscripted variables, FOCAL and BASIC can be applied to problems of considerably greater complexity.

Teaching Advanced Planning

The students' performances in developing their projects probably provide the most information about the efficacy of this pilot course in programming for children. Although the entire course was geared toward encouraging student initiative in a relatively free atmosphere, the course project was the first assignment which required a student to act independently in conceiving of a complex computer program. Overall, the children responded quite well to this challenge. The level of sophistication of the project programs suggests that children can become rather fluent in a computer programming language following a course of the kind outlined here. However, the course could probably be improved if it better communicated the importance of advanced planning for complex programs. The children undertook rather ambitious projects and initially believed that these programs could be composed within a few sessions at the terminals. Such a belief is not surprising in view of the fact that the programs prescribed in the manuals were usually simple enough to be composed within a single session at the lab. The projects, however, required many programming steps, and oftentimes many subroutines had to be assembled to complete these programs. Thus, when the children attempted to complete one part of the project program without anticipating the requirements of other portions of the program, they experienced some difficulties. To reduce this problem, the teacher asked the students to write out some general plans for their projects before they came to the lab. The procedure proved to be moderately successful in promoting more independent thinking and better student preparation.

Future revisions of the computer manuals for children should probably emphasize the need for planfulness by presenting the children with some problems intermediate in difficulty to the exercises currently used in the manuals and the more complex project programs. This should stimulate advanced organization of programs early in the course. In addition, the students should be taught appropriate heuristics (e.g., flow-charting) to assist them in anticipating the requirements of their programs. Such an emphasis on planning should facilitate the children's programming skills and may even generalize the other problem-solving situations.

References

Dwyer, T. A. "Heuristic Strategies for Using Computers to Enrich Education", *International Journal of Man-Machine Studies*, 1974, 6, 137-154.

Dwyer, T. A. "Soloworks: Computer-Based Laboratories for High School Mathematics", *School Science and Mathematics*, January 1975.

Feurzeig, W., R. Grant, G. Lukas and J. D. Lukas, *Programming Languages as a Conceptual Framework for Teaching Mathematics* (Vol. 1), Report No. 2165. Cambridge, Mass.: Bolt, Beranek and Newman, 1971. (ERIC No. ED057579, NTIS No. PB-206919.)

Roman, R. A. and J. I. Heller. *LOGO: A Student Manual*. Learning Research and Development Center, University of Pittsburgh, 1974.

Spencer, D. D. *Game Playing With Computers*. Rochelle Park, N.J.: Hayden, 1968.

THE AUTHOR TELLS, IN THE NEXT ARTICLE, ABOUT A STUDENT LEADERSHIP SYSTEM IN WHICH THIRD GRADERS MANAGE SKILLS WORKSHOPS AND INTEREST AREAS. THE LEADERSHIP SYSTEM ALLOWS YOUNGSTERS TO DEVELOP SELF-RELIANCE, TO THINK CREATIVELY AND TO TAKE ON MORE RESPONSIBILITY FOR THEIR LEARNING. THE AUTHOR DESCRIBES HOW SHE DESIGNED AND WORKED OUT A STUDENT LEADERSHIP PROGRAM IN HER OWN CLASSROOM.

CLASSROOM MANAGEMENT
BY AND FOR KIDS

Valdora Y. Freeman

Do you feel you must make a superhuman stretch to be "everything to every student"?

Are you confronted with large classes of youngsters who have such a wide range of interests and abilities that it seems impossible to meet all their needs?

Have you discovered that some of your students are self-motivated and resourceful enough to cope with and benefit from a semi-structured classroom, while others seem to require a great deal of structure?

Do you have fewer teacher aides and less support from specialists than you've had in the past?

Is the time you could previously allot to individual children or small groups now at a minimum?

Are you wondering which way to turn?

I was and, to some extent, still am. But I have worked out a student leadership system in my third grade that has been a tremendous help. In the past five years, it has greatly alleviated class design and management problems and enriched and enlivened our classroom routine.

Playing "Teacher"

The system is a takeoff on the idea of playing "teacher." It provides youngsters with the opportunity to be leaders of skills workshops and managers of interest areas set up in the classroom. Since the kids take on a great deal of responsibility for their own learning, I can afford to spend time on individualized instruction and meet their wide variations in learning styles by offering a program that is wide in scope.

The skills workshops cover assigned work and textbook lessons in all curriculum areas. The interest areas are in social studies; science; art, audio area; math, music; buddy area (the built-in drill system); library; language and theater; mini-theater, film lab and mini-publishing company; woodshop, custodial and safety area; "what's in the news."

The leadership program helps many aggressive students learn to channel their leadership abilities. Shy children improve their self-confidence and thus show remarkable personal growth. Others who have difficulty with their academic work display an amazing potential for leadership. Almost everyone shows improvement in creative and critical thinking skills, language fluency and self-image.

At the beginning of each day, workshop leaders are chosen alphabetically until all the children get a chance at these roles. The interest area managers are all volunteers. In the beginning of the year, we discuss the content of the interest areas, and the kids sign up for those areas they are most interested in. A few are very popular, and some students have to settle for their second choices. But before the discussion is over, everyone finds an area in which to serve, so that each one has two to four managers. Twice during the school year the children switch areas if they want to.

Skills Workshop Leaders

Our skills workshops are held every day. Students find which workshops they will be in for the day by looking for their names on one of several charts. A sliding red arrow indicates the leader. Below the chart are the required assignment for the day and a list of needed materials.

Each child participates in three or four skills workshops each day, traveling with one of the four flexible reading groups I assign early in the year. The reading groups rotate among the workshops each day. For example, on Monday, group A may go to Workshop 4 (audio area), Workshop 7 (buddy area) and Workshop 9 (language arts). On the same day, groups B, C and D each attend three of the other nine workshops. Every day, each group goes to a different set of workshops. Friday the cycle starts again.

On a typical day we start with whole-class participation in games or puzzles, or the children read for enjoyment or information. During this time the workshop leaders check their assignment charts, collect and look over the materials and meet with me or a volunteer aide if there are any questions. The interest area managers occasionally meet during this time, too, to plan activities.

Then, we hold a class meeting in the middle of the room to discuss current or future projects and exercise to relax. Afterwards, the children work on individual math assignments within their math groups. They are assigned to these groups in the same way that they are for reading. I conduct these lessons myself, because I feel the children need more of my immediate attention in this area than they do in the other subjects.

When the math work is completed, the leaders call their groups to a specific area, depending on the nature of the assignment, and start the day's workshops. For example, the science skills workshop is held in the science interest area. I move from group to group to check on the children's progress and help with individual problems. When I leave a group, the student leader takes over again. At the end of the day, the leaders distribute homework materials to their groups.

Area Interest Managers

Early in the afternoon, when our skills workshops are finished for the day, all the children visit the class "Selection Tree," a bulletin board display. They place small name tags on branches that are labeled with the interest areas to indicate which ones they want to work in. At the appropriate time, they go to the interest areas they have chosen and work on activities that the area managers have set up. The managers sometimes supervise activities and when they do, it is on a rotating basis.

The managers plan activities for their areas, usually research projects, team quizzes or games, but often their ideas are more ambitious. For example, the language area managers may organize and supervise rehearsals for original playlets and puppet or shadow shows for the whole class.

The managers' duties include overseeing their areas, reporting to me when supplies are low, keeping an eye on student participation and helping clean up. When special topics are brought up and explored by the whole class, the managers search for and display related books from the school and class libraries.

They are often called on to lead class discussions and question-and-answer periods. For example, a science film would be introduced and followed up with a discussion session by the science area managers. In the beginning of the year, the children are usually not very adept at this, but with guidance and practice, they become quite skilled as the year progresses.

One of the managers' special jobs is to write invitations to guest speakers. Following their acceptance, the managers send a list of questions from classmates to the guest to answer during the visit, serve as hosts and later write thank-you notes. Most of our guests are parents, but many visitors are from the school system or the community.

In addition, the managers keep a written record of each area's activities and guest visits, which they read orally during class meetings. They summarize this information semi-annually and together compile class newsletters, which also include original drawings, photos, riddles, games and puzzles.

Room Organization

The classroom design that works best for you will depend on your teaching methods and your students' learning styles. I have experimented with a couple of arrangements since different classes often warrant a change in structure.

In one arrangement, I set up the interest areas around the room's perimeter. I use large pieces of fiberboard as dividers that also hold hooked-on materials the children can reach easily, so that interruptions to get supplies are at a minimum. Desks, tables and small bookshelves containing specific materials are placed in each area in front of bulletin boards. The children's personal belongings are kept in individual cubbies. The center rug area is free for our frequent class meetings.

Another arrangement we have tried places the children's desks in the form of a horseshoe or similar shape facing the chalkboard. The interest areas are set up along the walls on a smaller scale than in the first arrangement. There is less space for meeting as a group in the center of the room, so we hold class meetings and group discussions from the desks. There is also less space for the interest areas, but all 12 do materialize with enough room to move around comfortably. Instead of using desks and tables in each area to work on projects, the children take available materials from each area back to their desks.

Areas and Activities

To organize your own room, you may want to select your own interest areas, based on the students' needs and abilities. Following is a list of areas we explore that may give you some ideas to get started.

AREA 1: PEOPLE, PLACES AND THINGS— SOCIAL STUDIES

A large round table and a small bookshelf containing children's social studies books, textbooks, games and map puzzles make up this area. I also include a "talking text," a tape of textbook sections for students who learn better aurally or who have difficulty reading. On a nearby bulletin board, I staple plastic pockets containing skills workshop worksheets, such as question-and-answer activities based on our text. Also included are maps and quizzes that students can use during interest area time.

This area's guests have included mail carriers, lawyers, truck drivers, travelers with slides and souvenirs to share, our school secretary, principal, a district ombudsperson who led the class in a discussion of class social problems and our superintendent of schools who talked about his job and hobbies.

AREA 2:   PROJECT DISCOVERY—SCIENCE

This area contains an oblong table, a small bookshelf full of science books and games, "talking texts" and a bulletin board with pockets containing science worksheets for the skills workshop and interest area. Also included are small cartons of experiment direction cards and equipment for individual or small-group experimentation. Special experiments are often set up by the area managers. Guests have included dentists, doctors, nurses and parents who introduced us to the "science" of cooking and preserving foods.

AREA 3:   ART

Four desks placed back to back to form a rectangle make up this area. In between the desks are fiberboard walls with slim shelves holding art supplies, such as scissors, thread, yarn, paints and brushes. On the sides of the wall we hang smocks and pockets to hold crayons, scrap materials, different kinds of paper and idea cards.

Art managers supply books on the master artists to share with classmates and present art films. They also plan a weekly theme for art projects. A sign in their areas reads, "What Can You Make From _____?" The managers insert, for example, "a cardboard roll," "pipe cleaners" or "vegetable trays." Classmates who would like to work with the featured material give it a try. When they are finished, the managers display the finished products and work with the students to think of ideas for class showcases and hall displays.

Guests have included sculptors, painters and a woman

from Japan who demonstrated origami. A local librarian showed us her handmade dollhouse and miniatures, which inspired several interested kids to construct a dollhouse.

AREA 4:   AUDIO AREA

A six-seat homemade carrel for listening activities is the backbone of this center. Taped lessons, which provide much of our basic skills work, are available for the work-shops on various subjects, such as spelling, math, language, creative writing and poetry. "Talking texts" and accompanying questionnaires are made up for social studies and science. Hooks on the walls of the carrel hold special follow-up cards and worksheets for buddy work and materials for the various lessons. During interest area time, the children also listen to taped stories, music or poetry.

AREA 5:   MATH

This area adjoins the end of the audio area, so that one side of the fiberboard is also used to hang math worksheets. There are also shelves to hold math games and materials for liquid and dry measurement. A very important part of this area is a liabrary of books on such topics as addition, subtraction, the history of math and computers. Guests have included storekeepers, accountants and computer workers. From time to time, the math managers hold addition, subtraction, multiplication and division bees.

AREA 6:   MUSIC

A piano and a long table containing a couple of xylophones, an autoharp and a hand organ make up our music corner. Other rhythm instruments are hung on a pegboard that has pockets to store sheet music, research fact sheets on the lives of famous composers, staff paper for original melodies and information sheets for learning notes. There are also a couple of music stands for duets and trios. The managers often plan whole-class entertainment on a sign-up basis, host programs with guest musicians and organize musical quizzes.

AREA 7: BUDDY AREA—THE BUILT-IN DRILL SYSTEM

Two or three pairs of desks that are each separated from the other by fiberboard walls make up the children's favorite part of the room for private study or teamwork. Hanging on the fiberboard walls are cards containing vocabulary and spelling words, alphabetizing activities, multiplication tables, social studies questions, scoring sheets and directions for buddy drillwork.

After completing their work at the audio area, the children are often assigned to the buddy area for follow-up assignments. Taking turns as student and leader, the buddy pairs quiz each other on a variety of subjects; such as spelling, social studies, number combinations and language. They also help each other study facts and prepare for class quizzes. Each leader keeps a record of his or her buddy's study needs. Many students return to this area at interest area time to practice particular lessons or review.

AREA 8: LIBRARY

Since our nonfiction class library books are located in the social studies, science and math areas, this area contains fiction primarily. It consists of several desks, bookshelves, book report forms and markers. Two filing cabinets contain the "talking book" library, recorded tapes of books on various subjects and poetry.

The managers keep track of the condition of the books and often supervise an early morning library time or book sharing time, when they call on classmates to review briefly books they have read or to act out parts. Guests have included our school librarian and bookmobile librarians.

AREA 9: LANGUAGE AND THEATER

This area consists of several desks arranged in front of a large piece of fiberboard. Pockets hung from the wall are used to hold handwriting practice materials; story-starter idea cards; sequence cards; flannel-backed paper and flannel letters and figures for word and sentence-building exercises and original scripts and booklets of short plays.

The managers often entertain the class with original

productions and put on shows for the younger grades, especially around the holidays. They also prepare language team quizzes. Guests have included authors and actors.

AREA 10:   MINI-THEATER, FILM LAB AND MINI-PUBLISHING COMPANY

This four-sectioned fiberboard carrel contains headsets, a mixing box, filmstrip viewers, recorders, blank cassettes, write-on film, a typewriter, typing paper, script and storyboard forms, slide mounts, blank 16mm photo leader, brown wrapping paper cut to size for opaque projector shows, rulers, scissors, pencil sharpeners and plastic film containers. The area is used regularly during the skills workshops for special taped lessons.

At interest area time, the children can make their own filmstrips in the film lab and show them in the mini-theater. Managers check on supplies, hold screening sessions of the student-made filmstrips and lead critique discussions. Occasionally, they award prizes for "best filmstrip of the year" after a class vote. [For more details on the mini-theater and film lab, see "An AV Center for Every Classroom," *Teacher*, May/June '76, p. 44.]

The mini-publishing company materials are typing paper, direction cards for bookmaking, binding materials and art supplies. The managers often oversee the binding process to make sure it's done correctly. A special shelf in the class library displays students' original books, which they share with each other and younger classes. Guests have included filmmakers from local audiovisual companies and authors.

AREA 11:   WOODSHOP, CUSTODIAL AND SAFETY AREA

In the corridor outside our classroom, we set up a large workbench with a variety of tools and hang pockets on the wall that contain woodworking plans. Before beginning any carpentry, the students must sketch the plans, noting all the measurements, and show them to the area managers. Guests have included our school custodian who demonstrated the uses of the tools and a carpenter who shared her expertise and assisted the children with their woodworking projects.

The custodial and safety managers are in charge of class cleanliness and safety. They arrange yearly visits from police officers, the school crossing guard, firefighters, construction workers and the custodian, who leads us on a tour of the boiler room.

AREA 12: WHAT'S IN THE NEWS

The center of our classroom is used by the news managers for class discussions of current newspaper articles. In addition to supervising these meetings, they hold weekly team quizzes. They also post articles on a small news bulletin board and distribute flyers announcing special TV programs or future class events, such as trips to local apple orchards, maple syrup farms and museum exhibits. Putting together a class newspaper covering area activities is an additional responsibility.

One particularly well-received guest was the education editor of our local newspaper. A staff photographer came with him to illustrate his presentation.

Open or Structured Classroom

If you are involved in making a switch from an open classroom to a "back to basics" organization, you'll find that a student leadership system will not only help smooth the transition but also provide you with time for individualized instruction. Or, if you have always utilized a more structured classroom, the system, even on a small scale, can be very compatible. It allows children to think creatively and develop their self-reliance. For us, it is a happy combination of ideas and action.

FOLLOWING IS AN ARTICLE THAT DISCUSSES HOW
PUPILS CAN SHARE IN PLANNING THEIR LEARNING
EXPERIENCES. THE SHARED PLANNING PROCESS
HELPS PUPILS TO BETTER PERCEIVE THE REASONS
AND PURPOSES FOR THEIR LEARNING. SEVERAL
GUIDELINES AND SUGGESTIONS ARE SET FORTH
FOR INCLUDING PUPILS IN SHARED CLASSROOM
PLANNING.

INCLUDING THE STUDENT IN
CLASSROOM MANAGEMENT

Devon J. Metzger

*Reprinted with permission from The Clearing
House, Vol. 54, No. 6 (February 1981), pp.
272-275. A publication of the Helen Dwight
Reid Educational Foundation.*

If classroom management persists as a problem, one of
the best ideas for improvement may be to let students help.
But there is a catch. A prerequisite to incorporating student
help is the teacher's view of students. We often overlook this
important and very basic aspect of classroom management.
The teacher's view of students can actually determine or
greatly influence how the teacher approaches classroom
management in general. This article supports the idea that
students now only can, but should, share responsibility
in their own formal learning experiences and thus directly
assist in the effective operation of the classroom. The following will further explore this idea and offer suggestions for
implementation.

Most educators witness dramatic contrasts in how
teachers view students. At one extreme are the teachers who

view the students as children incapable of acting or thinking without some direction from them. The students in turn learn to accept such a relationship as law. They soon learn to give up their individuality, independence and initiative and rely on the teacher to determine their educational identities. The result often is students who are unable and unwilling to act effectively and constructively or to learn without this external direction. The implications for learning and life in general are obvious and certainly are not compatible to a democratic society which requires participation and responsible decision making. At the other extreme is the teacher who forgets or chooses to abdicate his or her part of the "partnership." In this approach some students often become frantic as they attempt to discover some direction or purpose in their schooling hours, while other students react by choosing to withdraw in the face of confusion and frustration.

Viewing students as partners in the learning process does not translate into either one of these extremes. Accepting students as partners recognizes the greater experience and knowledge of the teacher, yet does not sacrifice the worth of the student as a human being nor ignore the ability of the student to assume more control over his or her life. The students are fully recognized as having individual needs, interests and abilities. The students are accepted as students, but within the larger context of being people. The students are viewed as emerging adults who must learn to make decisions and develop responsibility for themselves and their actions. Such a view is consistent with our educational purposes operating within a democratic context. A cornerstone of our democratic society is a participating citizenry. Learning to participate through responsible individual decision making is thus a critical skill and process for students to learn.

More specifically, accepting the view that students are capable suggests a sharing relationship or partnership within the classroom. In other words, teachers are expecting the students to be partners in the challenge of creating and maintaining a positive classroom environment. Be careful. For too many teachers, this means shifting the "burden" of discipline

96

to the students. Obviously this immediately suggests problems. Integral to this approach is a positive rather than a negative transition to shared responsibility. Requiring and/or dictating the new responsibility is much different from helping the students gradually learn to appreciate and welcome the change. After all, learning the concept of rights and responsibilities is developed in part through maturation. Helping students to appreciate and consequently accept responsibility in the classroom takes time, patience and knowledge to effectively facilitate this emerging ability. The following are guidelines and suggestions to help in this task.

Learn To Know Your Students

Learning to know each student, his or her own interests, needs and abilities, is a requirement to successfully implementing a teacher-student partnership in learning. Certainly, some limitations are involved in learning to know your students. Class size presents one of the greatest obstacles. Nevertheless, there is a variety of ways which can be utilized in helping teachers learn to know their students better. Requiring and using time to chat with the student during informal classroom activities or taking advantage of out-of-class time to visit with the student can help one develop a familiarity with students. However, the task is too important to leave to such informal means altogether. A systematic effort is better suited to and more efficient for gleaning information about students.

Using values clarification exercises is one of the best methods for doing this.[1] Such values clarification activities as forced ranking, rating sheets, and boundary breakers are appropriate. Also interest and inventory biography activities can help teachers to realize the interests and backgrounds of their students. Of course, a variety of pre-tests as well as the school's diagnostic services can be properly used to assess the students' academic abilities. The shortage of time may seem to work against efforts to know students well, but if teachers accept as an important goal learning to know their students, time can be found and legitimately utilized within our educational purposes.

Goal Flexibility

One of the most difficult habits for teachers to break is that of relying completely upon tradition. In this instance, tradition translates into a teacher's compulsion to follow the textbook closely. The fact is that using the textbook can be easier and safer than ignoring it altogether. However, as more teachers realize the limitations of the textbook, they find themselves increasingly comfortable in using it as a resource and not the sole source. This change can allow the teacher to spend more time and give more emphasis to individual student needs, interests and abilities. Learning to recognize the importance of goal flexibility—the ability to look beyond the class as a whole and match goals with individual needs and differences is an important step.

Essentially two approaches to practicing goal flexibility are available—"the same goal, different means approach." Schools include certain standard curriculum goals and objectives. Achieving the established goals can often be more effective when different means are used. When more freedom is allowed in curriculum planning, a general purpose is necessary, but different goals followed by different means can strongly facilitate a teacher-student partnership in the learning program. The teacher who has a larger sense of his or her purpose in the educational setting can more comfortably make a commitment to goal flexibility. It is usually such teachers who view students as capable of sharing in their own learning experiences.

Realistic Expectations

As indicated earlier, the inclusion of students as partners in the planning of their learning experiences is not necessarily an easy task. Both maturation and conditioning are factors involved in students' accepting new responsibilities. As students grow older, they naturally accept increasing responsibility for their own lives. Included in this process is a growing awareness and questioning of their formal education. Sometimes this emerging awareness is seen as threatening to the established order, or in this instance, to the daily classroom organization, subject matter or general school routine. However, the pupils' growing awareness of themselves and their ability to make decisions can be used to enhance their learning experiences.

Perhaps the factor which inhibits greater student responsibility in the learning program more than any other is conditioning. It is no secret that schools foster dependent learners—learners who learn to rely upon authority to direct their learning. Learning can become unpleasant and the removal of any teacher authority often results in a voluntary reaction against continuing to broaden one's knowledge conscientiously.

Consequently, easing students from a learner-dependent relationship to a partnership role can be a difficult and frustrating challenge. It is important to provide opportunities for students to learn gradually to accept and become comfortable with this new arrangement. And remembering that students are different means that some students will take longer than others to accept and appreciate this new role of increased responsibility in the learning process. Most students will readily accept the responsibility once they recognize it is authentic and not just another ploy to inspire work. Using the carrot approach can be especially useful in facilitating the transition to a teacher-student partnership. In this approach students who are more ready to accept and act as partners are given the opportunities to pursue and utilize the new learning arrangement. As the advantages are witnessed by other students, the prerequisite agreement to accept new privileges and their accompanying responsibilities becomes attractive. Gradually all students can be pulled or gently pushed into sharing responsibility for their own learning experiences.

Expanding the Role of Students

Along with including students in the goal-setting process, it is important to remember that their partnership can extend into other areas. Involving students in the learning program can include their participating in record keeping, evaluation, and learning to assist and learn from their peers.

Accepting the premise that students are capable of

participating in their own learning includes expanding their responsibilities into other areas. Teachers have long been burdened with excessive record keeping. Yet there seems little reason to think students are not capable of sharing in this task as part of their larger partnership role. Charting their own progress, reporting on their project accomplishments and checking deadlines can become a student's habit as well as a teacher's habit. Likewise, students can learn to devise methods of evaluating their performance which can become a part of program planning. Instead of the usual group testing, individual students can prepare ways of presenting their progress. Oral testing and project presentations provide two ways of making evaluation more flexible and also of including students in the process. Teaching students to evaluate their own progress is clearly a valuable example of having students share in their own learning. Students who are able to identify their own strengths and confront realistically their own limitations are involved in important learning experiences.

Another measure which serves several advantages is that of teaching students to assist one another in learning. Students can learn the responsibility of aiding one another instead of engaging in the sort of competition which often detracts from authentic learning.[2] As the atmosphere of cooperation develops through the partnership-in-learning role, students can become more comfortable in providing assistance for one another.

The Teacher's Changing Role

Accepting that pupils are capable and can share in their learning experiences assumes more than a change for the students. Taking a first step often leads to a journey much further than expected. As students grow used to sharing in the planning of their learning, they will come to expect such involvement. Your role as teacher will change from the role you originally expected or were trained for. As a partner in learning, you become a facilitator, an organizer, an arranger of the learning environment. You may also become an information source; but if you are successful, you will only be one of the information sources. Along with this role change, you will want to be prepared to give students more space and freedom of movement. Remember—along with responsibilities also come rights and privileges. In time your classroom may become the center of learning, a check-in-point, a resource center or simply a place where you are if help or direction are needed. Recognizing this probable change can allow you to prepare for it. Several suggestions can be made here. Developing a good relationship with the school librarian is one way to prepare. The librarian can become a team-teacher with you in some endeavors. Including the librarian in your class goals and advising him or her about individual student goals allows the librarian to help the student more efficiently. Most librarians are delighted to be included in such planning. This enables them to serve the school in the way they were trained to. Also, a planned systematic use of the library and librarian gives you another classroom and a competent co-worker. Along with this approach, you may want to try to have your room as close to the library as possible to facilitate its use further. This causes fewer problems as students move to and from the library freely. In addition, find free rooms at different periods near your classroom to use as temporary quiet centers or rooms to set up media presentations for individual students or groups of students. Likewise, spot nooks and crannies about the school which can provide places for individual student study. Having a friendly relationship with the custodian of the school can help you in this task; e.g., finding extra chairs to use under stairwells or cleaning out unused or partially used storerooms.

It is important here to re-emphasize how students gradually learn to share in the learning program. You may have visions of students roaming about the school scattered in every free room and space. This could happen, but it takes time and it can be a slow process in which students often one by one accept the responsibility/rights concept. Your flexible approach must also gain credibility with the principal and other teachers. You may also feel uncomfortable at some point with this new student freedom. If so, you will need to draw your own boundaries, perhaps with students involved in

101

the decision. However, it is likely your students will develop a responsible reputation which comfortably allows you to utilize the entire school and school grounds as your class-room. Again, you must ask yourself how you view students.

In conclusion, what is being emphasized is the premise that students are capable of sharing in their own formal learning. Accepting this view, it is hypothesized that class-room management can be positively influenced both directly and indirectly. As students become partners in the learning experience, they accept responsibilities. As students help develop their own goals and objectives, they buy into their own success and, indirectly, into that of the larger classroom community. By being flexible and expanding learning goals and objectives, students can more easily see the reasons and purposes for learning. These understandings naturally involve them in a new commitment to themselves, the teacher, and their peers. Classroom management can improve from such a shared planning and learning experience, and the reality of authentic participation contributes to a positive classroom atmosphere and to meaningful learning experiences.

References

[1]For a wealth of values clarification examples, see Louis Raths, Merrill Harmin and Sidney Simon, *Values and Teaching*, Second Edition. Cleveland, OH: Charles Merrill Publishing Company, 1978.

[2]See Arthur W. Combs, *Myths in Education* Boston: Allyn and Bacon, Inc., 1979, Part 1, to help explore the myth of competition which works against students helping and learning from each other.

THE ARTICLE THAT FOLLOWS DESCRIBES TWO STU-
DENT-INITIATED VIDEO PROJECTS. THESE PROJECTS,
WHICH PROVIDED FOR CONSIDERABLE STUDENT
CREATIVITY, RESULTED IN SUCCESSFUL AND
WORTHWHILE LEARNING. THE AUTHOR TELLS HOW
STUDENTS PARTICIPATED IN FORMULATING PLANS
AND ESTABLISHING GOALS FOR THE PROJECTS.

LET THE STUDENTS SET THE GOALS

Carol C. Kuhlthau

*Reprinted from Instructional Innovator, Vol. 26,
No. 3 (March 1981), pp. 28-29, by permission of
the Association for Educational Communications
and Technology.*

When several students on the audiovisual crew at the
high school where I was media specialist approached me with
the idea of forming a newscast staff to videotape school
news, I hesitated. Their plan was ambitious: they proposed
to tape interviews, school activities, and special events, and
to show the videotapes to other students in the commons
during lunch periods.

Often student-initiated projects of this type crop up
during the school year at the most inopportune moments—
after plans have been formulated and goals established—and
this one was no exception. Furthermore, there were all the
usual reasons that the project was impractical: lack of funds,
equipment, personnel, and time.

Reservations

Although the school was a new, multimillion-dollar

103

complex with provision for a closed-circuit television system and television production studio, these facilities were all in the future. A recently completed five-year plan for the video program provided for gradual acquisition of equipment each year.

The technician also was in the five-year plan. With no technician to help with equipment malfunctions or production techniques, my policy had been to keep the video program simple.

Time would be a pressing problem, too. The audiovisual crew was a service club, an extracurricular activity rather than a journalism class meeting daily. The students would have to do all the work after school, during lunch, or in study periods.

Also, the audiovisual crew had been organized to assist in meeting the objectives of the existing video program —to provide ITV programs to teachers and to videotape classes when teachers requested. The crew also helped with circulation and operation of other audiovisual equipment.

So I hesitated. Then I realized that our five-year plan of gradual growth meant little to the present crew. In five years they would have graduated and gone their separate ways.

I decided to let them try the project. The result was exciting, productive work that accomplished both the institutional objectives of the existing video program and the students' objectives for the newscast project.

Spontaneity Is The Key

How often institutional goals shut out possibilities for individuals to initiate tasks! Yet some of the most meaningful (and memorable) experiences for students are those that parallel the programs that the school has established. As the newscast project moved from planning to shooting to editing, these students learned from both their successes and their failures.

From the many ideas that were spontaneously suggested, the crew selected several stories on a variety of topics to start with. One would interview the officers of each class to find out what they had accomplished and what their future plans were. Another would talk with the sports coaches and tape some practices and games. A third would interview seniors in the senior lounge (at the time, there was some controversy about this special privilege). Yet another would interview the director of the school play and tape a portion of the dress rehearsal.

The students quickly realized that they needed to work in teams of three—a reporter and two technicians, one to operate the camera and the other to set up sound, lighting, and wiring. The reporters took the responsibility for preliminary scheduling to arrange interviews and taping sessions and then to inform the technicians.

After a few videotaping sessions, the crew discovered some ways to avoid disappointments and time-consuming retakes. The videotapes improved when the reporters began to prepare loose scripts of the scenes and review them with the technicians. Loose scripting gave a sense of direction and purpose, yet allowed for spontaneity and unexpected contingencies.

Editing was a major task, and the problems that arose seemed insurmountable. After many frustrating hours, the students decided that the solution was to videotape carefully, so that there would be little or no editing within segments. The student editors needed only to retape the separate segments onto one videotape, and to tape the title and credits with background music onto the beginning of the final tape.

When the newscast staff premiered the completed videotape, they were delighted with its reception. Their colleagues crowded around the television set, watching intently, laughing, and waiting to see themselves and their friends on the screen. Their greatest reward, though, was the sense of accomplishment in having worked through the obstacles to complete a presentation that they themselves had initiated.

This project continued for the rest of the school year, with the students making one newscast a month.

Students Must Be Motivators

The newscast project had been so successful that I incorporated it into the video program's goals for the next year. I called the audiovisual crew together to announce that we would be bigger and better, with a newscast every two weeks instead of once a month, and with more professional quality.

Now, however, the goals were no longer the students'. Many who had worked on the news the previous year had graduated; others had just gone on to other activities. The remaining crew members and the new recruits tried, but the spark was gone. The project was not inner-motivated. We turned to other things.

As an outgrowth of the newscasts, however, another student-initiated project surfaced that turned out to be equally creative and innovative. A small group of students proposed to videotape some humorous pieces of high school life, something of an underground newscast.

Their ideas provoked the same reservations as before— and an additional one: Would they make a statement that the administration would strongly oppose? Again, my reservations proved unfounded. The students carefully planned a satirical statement that contained both critical analysis and genuine affection. The teachers were surprisingly cooperative when they were the targets of spoofs. After the tape was completed, we enjoyed a healthy, hearty laugh at ourselves.

Teacher as Adviser

The teacher's role in student-initiated projects is not the traditional one of defining goals and designing activities that enable students to meet these goals. The students take on this role, and maintain control throughout the project.

Supervision is necessary to the success of such projects, but it must be unstructured. The teacher acts as an adviser, with the roles of trouble-shooter, messenger, and expediter.

The troubleshooter needs the sensitivity to know when to step in, and when to step aside. When students meet an insurmountable block, the adviser does whatever is necessary to get things going again. That may mean working long hours with one group on its part of the project.

The messenger role in these projects was crucial. The students didn't meet regularly in a class, so I became the messenger or gatekeeper. Students would stop by the media center to leave or pick up messages. Without this service the projects would have faltered for lack of communication.

The expediter role is actually that of "gofer." Students working along on a project may find that they need an item they don't have, and the adviser may be the only person able to find it and deliver it.

The students are involved in the exciting, creative, rewarding work and the teacher is assisting in the nitty-gritty, often frustrating, but necessary backup tasks. The students are the initiators, the coordinators, and the culminators.

A differentiation of student roles evolved early in the planning sessions of these video projects. One strong leader emerged who set the tone, pace, and structure for both the group and the project. Several co-leaders assisted the leader, or became leaders of subgroups working on different aspects of the project. Some students were willing to follow the direction of the leaders, but they also were active participants making significant contributions. Finally, some were culminators who pulled together the loose ends and completed the work of the entire group.

Build in Flexibility

The school program needs to be sufficiently flexible to leave space for students to initiate their own undertakings and formulate their own goals. This is not to suggest abandoning long- and short-range planning, but rather maintaining a degree of calculated openness, to allow for spontaneous student-initiated projects.

In these two video projects, exciting and creative work, as well as significant learning took place. They convinced me of the value of keeping programs flexible, and I now wait with calculated openness for forthcoming projects initiated by students.

THE AUTHOR OF THE NEXT ARTICLE DISCUSSES
STUDENT-PLANNED INDIVIDUALIZED LEARNING
PROGRAMS. THESE PROGRAMS HELP STUDENTS TO
LEARN HOW TO LEARN, AND TO BECOME MORE
SELF-DIRECTED. SEVERAL GUIDELINES AND PRO-
CEDURES ARE PRESENTED FOR INVOLVING STU-
DENTS IN PLANNING THEIR LEARNING EXPERIENCES.

INDIVIDUALIZED LEARNING:
STUDENTS CAN DO THEIR OWN PLANNING

Barry K. Beyer

Reprinted with permission from The Clearing House, Vol. 55, No. 2 (October 1981), pp. 61-64. A publication of the Helen Dwight Reid Educational Foundation.

For years school administrators and classroom teachers have been concerned with devising learning experiences and programs tailored specifically to the individual interests, learning styles, and abilities of the wide variety of students they find in their classrooms. The current attention devoted to developing special learning programs for exceptional children—especially those labeled as gifted and talented—has aroused new interest in ways to accomplish this goal. One result of this interest has been a renewed attention to various ways of individualizing learning. And rightly so, because individualized learning proves highly effective for such students.

In spite of its obvious benefits, many educators shun individualized learning. Most object to it largely on the grounds that a great amount of time is required of teachers and administrators to plan and prepare the individual programs which distinguish this type of learning. And there is no doubt that individualized learning, as traditionally implemented, does require considerable teacher time. But this need not be so.

Students can plan their own individual learning experiences and they can do it as an integral part of their own regular classroom learning. By having students plan their own study programs in this way we can eliminate the need for teachers and administrators to devote considerable time to such tasks prior to the start of school. Furthermore, by making student-planning part of their own classroom learning rather than antecedent to it or apart from it, we can use classroom instruction as a way for students to learn how to learn as well as to learn specific subjects.

This article outlines how these two goals can be accomplished. It identifies three basic guidelines and some procedures that can be used to implement student-planned individualized learning in any subject in intermediate and secondary grades.

Guidelines for Student-Individualized Learning

Involving students in planning their own learning programs is neither difficult nor excessively time consuming. It can be done well if we accept the following three assertions and their corollary guidelines.

First, individualized learning does not require that all students start their study on an individual basis from the very first day of school. Instead, all students eligible for such study can begin the school year in a single conventionally taught class to master a common core of knowledge and skills related to individualized learning. Such a class can also give them supervised practice in completing individualized, self-paced learning activities. Once these twin goals have been accomplished, these students can then plan and launch their own self-devised individual learning programs.

A common core experience for students scheduled to embark on individual study might consist of specific content designed to broaden student horizons or pique student curiosity in the physical sciences, the arts, the social sciences and/or the humanities. It might also consist of learning about the resources available for study in their school and community. Such a core might even consist of learning various learning skills such as problem solving—starting, for example, with how to identify, select, and delimit a problem, how to invent and test alternative solutions, and so on. Ideally, such a core experience might integrate all those types of learning into a meaningful basis for further independent learning.

Furthermore, part of this common core can be presented in an individualized format, thus giving students guided experience in the self-paced, individual study similar to what they will be expected to undertake later in the semester. Not all students are self-starters, as we know. And not all are experienced at the self-directed learning that is an essential feature of individualized learning. By offering some units of study in a core class as individual study units, students gain experience with it before they are left to do it on their own. For example, after a week or so of a conventionally taught class, have each student complete a short unit at his or her own pace but by a specific deadline; next, all students could reconvene as a conventional class for a few days to discuss how they did what they did in this unit, after which each could try another short, individualized unit. Following a rather short, common debriefing of techniques and skills useful in independent study, the students could then begin planning their own individual study programs.

Second, individualized learning need not be a program complete in and of itself. Very often we individualize an entire course so that a student essentially moves at his or her own rate of speed—or according to some set schedule— through a set of teacher-designed units or projects without any formal classes or other group instruction. In such a case, the individualized experience may stand by itself. But this pattern need not be the only one we use.

Individualized study can parallel, precede, or follow common, more conventional learning experiences. For example, a student could study in sequence a number of units or projects on his or her own while simultaneously preparing for and participating in one regularly scheduled small group discussion every second week or so with other students also engaged in individual study. These students could also attend a required monthly lecture or large group presentation. Or they may attend a common class that meets two or three times weekly while each completes a series of individual projects during the other days when the class does not meet. Another option is that student may share a common class experience, then proceed individually in their own study reconvening periodically in small, task-oriented groups to share or apply what they have learned on their own. Individualized study may thus be a course complete in itself, only one of a variety of components of a single course, or merely a supplement to some other form of study.

Third, individualizing learning does not necessarily mean that students must work by themselves all the time. While such study does permit maximum flexibility for individual growth, it often inhibits the kind of peer interaction that stimulates the creative and reflective thinking so essential to human development. Some student learning, even in individualized programs, may thus be devised for pairs of students or for triads or small groups. Such cooperative activities might be particularly useful to:

- launch an individualized unit or course.

- provide periodic reviews at designated places in a course or semester, or

- provide students opportunities to share and apply what they have been learning on their own to a common problem or task.

This departure from completely individual learning need not interrupt the progress of individual students on their own programs, for joint activities can parallel basic individual study. Moreover, even when students prepare joint projects or reports, the students in a group can be tested individually to determine individual progress.

By incorporating some team learning into an individualized program of study, students can thus receive the benefits of teaching each other and learning from others. They can also develop some of the precious social interaction skills that require practice and development throughout an entire course.

Student-Designed Programs

Most individualized learning units, courses, or programs such as LAPs, contracts, and self-paced (personalized) instruction programs are prepared exclusively by teachers. These programs consist frequently of elaborate sets of instructions, collections of study materials, and even progress tests. They prove especially valuable where students must learn a predetermined body of knowledge or set of skills.

But students can design their own individualized learning programs, too. Given an outline similar to that on the following page, a student—with a teacher's assistance as needed—can generate a personal study plan. This plan can help a student to explore individual interests in a more open-ended and relevant way than typifies most teacher-designed individual programs. The planning outline presented here requires a student to attend to all the ingredients of a useful learning activity, including goals, objectives, procedures, key materials to be used, evaluation criteria, and schedule. Adaptations of this outline may serve many different types of individualized learning programs. Student planning with the aid of this outline will prove especially effective after students have completed several teacher-made learning units that follow approximately the same format as the students are to use in their individual plans.

The procedure for implementing such student planning can be accomplished in the common class in which all students pursuing the individualized program are enrolled. They may first study the common core skills and content of this class by engaging in group activities guided by teacher-made individualized study guides similar in format to the programs the students will later design for themselves. Then, the students alone or in small groups can generate their own programs for study using the outline form presented here. They can share initial drafts of their proposals with each other for

STUDENT PLANNING GUIDE

DIRECTIONS: Complete the following in duplicate. Be sure you discuss this project with your teacher and secure the teacher's signature <u>before</u> beginning this study.

1. Write here a topic or subject about which you wish to know more:

2. Tell <u>why</u> you want to investigate this topic:

3. List as clearly as possible three things you propose to learn, find out or be able to do, write or speak about by investigating this topic or subject:
   a)
   b)
   c)

4. List the main steps by which you propose to accomplish the above objectives.
   a) First, I will . . .   d) . . .

   b) Next, I will . . .   e) Finally, I will . . .

   c) . . .

5. List here at least 3 specific sources or materials you can use that <u>may</u> be helpful in accomplishing your main objectives:
   a)

   b)

6. Tell at least 3 things you propose to do—and how well you propose to do them—to demonstrate that you have accomplished the objectives listed in # 3 above:
   a)

   b)

   c)

7. Indicate the amount of time you expect to devote to this project and the schedule you will follow:
   a) time:
   b) schedule:

   *starting date: *progress reporting date:

   *progress reporting date: *final evaluation date:

Instructor's signature   **Date**   **Your signature**

114

informative feedback. They can submit revised proposals to the teacher for revisions or approval. Brief exploratory study of the subjects of their proposed studies may be undertaken in the course of this process. But finally, when both teacher and student agree to the provisions of the proposal, they may sign it in each other's presence, each retaining a copy. At this point, students are ready to launch their individual programs. Almost.

When a student proposal contains a number of distinct goals, the student should prepare a plan for accomplishing each goal. The planning outline presented here may be adapted for this purpose. The student should break the overall proposal into distinct chunks or units, each built around a specific major goal. The procedure for planning these smaller units of study can be similar to the procedure used for planning the overall proposal. When a unit plan is approved and completed, the student can then prepare a plan for accomplishing another goal of the main proposal. This procedure of planning-doing-reporting-evaluating can be repeated for each goal in the overall proposal. Such a procedure produces study units of reasonable length, ensures steady student progress, and encourages periodic student-teacher interaction throughout the learning experience.

Summary

Individualized learning offers one effective way to reach exceptional students. Such learning may occur in a variety of formats. Students can propose their own individual programs using procedures outlined in this article. When students are involved in planning their own learning programs, the procedure can become part of the student learning process itself rather than being viewed as teacher preparation time outside of this experience.

Individualizing learning has many other benefits, too. It sharpens teacher and student awareness of the ingredients of good teaching, especially of the need for congruence among objectives, materials, learning procedures, and evaluation. It enables individual students to capitalize on and deepen their own interests and abilities while also discovering and developing other interests and abilities. When individualized learning involves the students in planning their own learning, it can teach them how to become self-directed learners, a goal of all formal education. This last benefit is, indeed, probably the most outstanding attribute of individualized learning and a very worthwhile reason for its use in our classroom today.

IN THE FINAL ARTICLE, THE AUTHOR TELLS HOW
PUPILS CAN BE DIRECTLY INVOLVED IN MAKING
DECISIONS CONCERNING THE DETERMINATION OF
OBJECTIVES, CONTENT, ACTIVITIES, MATERIALS
AND EVALUATION DEVICES. THE PUPILS, THROUGH
PARTICIPATING IN PUPIL-TEACHER DECISION MAK-
ING, LEARN TO DEFINE PROBLEMS, SUGGEST AND
FORMULATE SOLUTIONS, CARRY OUT PLANS AND
EVALUATE RESULTS. THE ARTICLE OFFERS SPECI-
FIC IDEAS FOR HELPING TEACHERS TO INVOLVE
PUPILS IN THE COOPERATIVE DECISION MAKING
PROCESS.

PUPIL-TEACHING DECISION MAKING

William J. Stewart

*Reprinted with permission from The Clearing
House, Vol. 56, No. 6 (February 1982), pp.
281-282. A publication of the Helen Dwight
Reid Educational Foundation.*

Pupil-teacher decision making enables pupils to be
actively and constructively involved in the classroom decision
making process. This concept embraces cooperative decision
making on the part of a teacher and a pupil, or teachers and
pupils, or between pupils. Pupil-teacher decision making is
not an end in itself, but a means toward individualizing instruction.

Individualizing instruction is based on the premise
that all pupils have unique combinations of abilities, interests, needs and ways of perceiving and responding. This idea
conflicts with traditional teaching practice in which the
teacher usually gives standardized lessons and expects uni-

form responses from all pupils. Essentially, in traditional practice, the pupils are expected to learn attitudes, concepts and skills by being fitted into a rigid teaching-learning "mold" prescribed exclusively by the teacher.

On the other hand, the teacher who individualizes instruction structures the class according to the unique differences of each pupil. Since the abilities, interests, needs and learning styles of each pupil differ widely, a great deal needs to be known about the pupils and their differences. To detect all the pupils' individual differences is an impossible task.

At this point, pupil-teacher decision making enters the picture. By allowing the pupils to participate in making decisions about objectives, content, activities, materials and evaluation devices, and by providing opportunities for them to express their interests, it is possible to accommodate their individual differences effectively.

Pupils can be involved in making decisions in connection with:

- A unit of work in any subject

- Independent study projects

- Discussion periods

- A day's, a week's, or a semester's plan of work

- A class or school activity (plans, projects, drives, programs, clubs, councils)

- Field trips

- Classroom or school behavior problems

- Room or school responsibilities

There are many benefits to be derived from pupil-teacher decision making. For example, the concept helps to develop social skills, promote democratic action, place the responsibility for learning on the pupils and promote independent thought and action. In addition, pupils learn to identify problems, think about these probems, suggest and plan for possible solutions, execute plans and evaluate outcomes.

The important phases of pupil-teacher decision making are set forth below:

- Why will this be done? The purposes, goals, objectives; the motivation of the unit, topic, or course; creating interests; identifying ends-in-view for individuals and groups.

- What is to be done? What research, what reading, what writing, what records to be kept, what activities, what projects? A unit, a week's work, a semester's work? The choices and the "musts".

- Who will do the jobs in question? Individuals, groups of pupils, the whole class.

- When will they be done? A calendar, a time schedule, the organization, the sequence.

- Where will they be done? In the classroom, laboratory, library, auditorium, on a field trip.

- How were they done? Continuous evaluation as the learning experience progresses, standards of achievement, improvements to be made.

The successful involvement of pupils in classroom decision making signifies that teachers have to:

- Be willing to let the pupils share in making decisions and to have a "piece of the action",

- See themselves as members of the group rather than the final authority on all topics,

- Free themselves of any feelings that the pupils

will "run the class"

- Be a helper and guide rather than merely a transmitter of facts,

- Create a relaxed classroom atmosphere in which the pupils feel secure in being themselves,

- Be accepting of all the pupils' responses and recognize that each response has legitimacy and worth.

Following are some suggestions for involving pupils in the classroom decision making process:

A sixth grade class is studying a unit on electromagnetism. A film that provides a general overview is used to introduce the electromagnetism unit. A planning period is then conducted in which the pupils are encouraged to ask questions about electromagnetism. Questions such as these might emerge:

- Why does a wire carrying an electric current act like a magnet?

- How can we tell which end of an electromagnet is the north-seeking pole?

- How are electromagnets used in industry? In the home?

The questions are written on the board and categorized under main headings. Individual and group situations are then formed, according to the pupils' interests, to seek answers to the various questions.

Another approach is for the teacher and pupils to discuss the unit objectives. The pupils then select objectives that they want to work on. The teacher also assigns objectives for the pupils to accomplish. The teacher and pupils then choose activities for achieving the objectives. Pupils who share the same objectives and activities work in appropriate large-group or small-group situations. Any pupil who is the only one involved with a particular objective and activity works in an individual situation.

At the beginning of each period in which the unit is being taught, the teacher and pupils plan what they will do during that period, This plan, usually simple, gives direction to the day's activities. In some cases, the plan is written on the board for the entire class. In other cases, the pupils prepare individual plans. The pupils' plans are also used as a basis for evaluating work. The plans are checked at the end of the period to see how well the pupils accomplished what they had set out to do and to determine what needs to be done the next period.

The computer can aid in faciliating pupil-teacher decision making. Statements of pupil interests and/or objectives, identified through teacher and/or pupil-teacher decision making, are first entered into the computer. The computer then generates suggestions or activities, materials and evaluation devices for individuals and groups in relation to such pupil variables as achievement level, mental age and reading level.

The computer can also be applied to adapt instruction to the pupils' learning styles. In this procedure, the computer initially produces a learning style profile which identifies, evaluates and prioritizes the types of activities through which an individual or a group learns best. For example, some pupils might learn most effectively through films, lectures and reading assignments; others through computer-assisted instruction, hands-on materials and workbooks; and still others through independent study projects, problem solving activities and simulations.

The computer, in formulating the learning style profile, analyzes, synthesizes and interprets pupil input through such sources as attitude scales, conferences, group discussions, interest inventories and questionnaires. The profile also embodies other pupil variables such as chronological age, mental age and reading level.

In actual practice, statements of interests and/or

objectives are entered into the computer, which in turn interacts with the pupil profile and ultimately generates suggestions of activities, materials and evaluation devices matched to the pupils' learning styles.

The teacher must thoroughly prepare for involving the pupils in making classroom decisions. As a result of this preparation, the teacher has many suggestions of activities to offer and a variety of materials ready for class use. In addition, the teacher has to be certain that:

- all pupils are involved with worthwhile objectives and activities;

- each pupil's abilities, interests and needs are being met;

- the pupils do not stray from their purposes;

- no important content is left out;

- the pupils participate in evaluating their own efforts.

Individualizing instruction cannot be truly effective unless pupil-teacher decision making is used as a means for identifying and meeting the requirements of each pupil. Selecting objectives, activities, materials and evaluation devices on the basis of individual abilities, interests and needs makes it possible to develop teaching-learning situations that bring maximum benefit to each pupil.